WHY DID WE MEET?

It Wasn't By Choice

SAMUEL P. HOLLOWAY III

© Copyright 2016 by Samuel P. Holloway III

All rights reserved. No part of this book may be reproduced or transmitted in any form or by any means, electronic or mechanical, including photocopying, recording, or by any information storage and retrieval system, without permission in writing from the publisher Samuel P. Holloway III at SPH3 Publishing, except in the case of brief quotations embodied in critical articles or reviews.

ISBN: 978-0-692-78860-8

10 9 8 7 6 5 4 3 2 1

Visit my website at

www.SamuelHolloway3.com

DEDICATION

I would like to dedicate this book to my nephews, nieces and great nieces. You all are my children through my siblings. I am doing all of this to ensure your safety I would give my life to ensure that what happened to me and the road I've traveled, you will never face. I love you all from the bottom of my heart and I never want any of you to suffer from the valley I walked through. When we know better we do better use my mistakes as a guide and learn from them. My Mission is to live in my TRUTH while trying to help others avoid my route or show them how to cope if otherwise! #KidsFirst #SaveOurYouth

ACKNOWLEDGEMENTS

First and foremost I want to give praise to the almighty creator without YOU, nothing is possible!

I want to send a special shout out to these individuals. Everyone has someone who motivates them and the people that motivate me are Dell Diane Miller, Franda Clay, Miayasha Harris and Nate' Billingsley-Walton.

Diane is my partner we handle business together and she is a real "Goal Getter" she encourages me to seek more.

Franda is the greatest teacher /professor there is she is someone who feeds me knowledge and advice whenever I need it.

Miayasha is my savior she helped me when I was at my lowest point in life.

Naté Billingsley-Walton you have no idea how much I love and admire you when I think of you tears come to my eyes you are my inspiration determination and motivation I love you so much from the bottom of my heart the core of my soul and baby you don't even know it!

These people have my back and I love them for it they will forever hold a special place within my heart. M U A H

THANK YOUS

I have to give thanks for those who've helped me with this project Damion Snowden for his poem, Regis Will for his photography and for the pictures for both book "How It All Happened" and this book, Jessica Godbee for creating this master piece with the cover, spine and back cover of all my books and Myron Schippers editing all my books too.

And an extra thank you to the victims whom came forward and telling their stories and for having the courage for speaking their truth, salute my queens!

TABLE OF CONTENTS

1. Why Did We Meet 1
2. Miami With the Bestie 14
3. Graduation Book Release Party 24
4. My Peace 40
5. My Judy On Duty 52
6. The Dating Scene 71
7. DL Men 86
8. My Neighbor 123
9. #26 & #14 135
10. Road Warriors 145
11. The Unheard Voices: All the Inbox Questions & Comments 156
12. College Life 182
13. Deuces 192
14. It Wasn't By Chance 208

NEVER GIVE UP

By Samuel P. Holloway III

People want to see me dead because they know someone who took me to bed.

People want to see me dead because they asked me for head.

People want to shut me up but I will never give up!

Some people said I lied and even JESUS was crucified.

Some people say I shouldn't have told but I did anyway now that I'm old.

Some people say I'm through and I said why didn't they sue?

Some people said I'm not right and I tell them, "I'm fighting with all my might!"

INTRODUCTION

Isn't life crazy? You can't go messing over GOD's children and not think it will come back to you. Everything done in the dark always comes to the light. How can you throw a stone and try to hide your hand after the fact?

Some of my molesters molested or raped someone before me and after me. So many people reached out that were victims to my molesters that it's insane. One of my molesters named Stacy Ray Whitt has 11 victims including me; he personally raped 5 women, molested 5 girls, one of whom is his niece.

How could these bastards get away with taking someone's innocence? How could Stacy Ray Whitt get away with this?! These were questions I needed answers to. If anything, I wanted to know what I could do to rectify the situation, not only for the other victims, but for myself and anyone else who has not come forward. I am not a victim anymore I'm not a little boy who didn't have a voice I'm an advocate seeking justice for people who can't speak for themselves. I am a voice for the "Silent Voices!" I am a man who is telling it all without any hesitation! Enough Is Enough!

I have thought about what if my life was different; what if everything I went through could be undone? The first thing would be my mom would never have given my sister away. I would have grown up knowing who my biological father was. I would not have been molested by mom's boyfriend. My mother wouldn't have beaten me when she found out. My two second cousins would not have had sex with me. My brother would not have started to beat me. My brother's seven friends would not have used me as a sex slave. My mother would not have started hating me and stopped loving me. Some of my family members would not have rejected me. I would not have gone through any bullying or fighting because I am gay. I would not have been raped. I would not have married a man that didn't love me or beat me. I would not have almost lost my life from the 3 men that tried to kill me over my ex-husband. And most importantly, I wouldn't be gay.

Unfortunately, that's not how life works and everything that happened was supposed to happen right when it did. If not for those events I would not be the ambitious, brave, courageous, loving, kind, strong person I am today. Everything happens for a reason and these horrific events shaped my life and made me better and not bitter. The road I've been down is dark, dangerous, curvy and beyond scary. All I am trying to do is prevent someone from taking the same route!

PROLOGUE

Some people thought because they sent me death threats I would stop talking and I would stop writing. Well, little did they know they became fuel to my fire I was neither going to be intimidated nor stop talking. I released all of my molester's names and with that, came their friends exposing themselves and I didn't even say a damn word, I just simply threw hints we all know only dogs bark when they are hit. Still to this very day 5 years after *Eyes Without A Face* The Story Of Samuel P. Holloway III, was released December 27, 2011 — NO LAWSUITS HAVE BEEN FILED! HA! … Who's lying?!

CHAPTER 1

WHY DID WE MEET

Who would have thought I would have fallen in love at the time I did. I put it out into the atmosphere I wanted a relationship I wasn't looking for love I wanted love to find me. Surely enough that's just what happened. It was unimaginable because I'm not attracted to dark-skin men at least that's what I thought!

I loved the light skinned brothers however my GOD had something different in store for me. I never thought I would ever feel this feeling again I thought the feeling of having real love actually went away with Price. Not to mention the thought of even wanting to get married again I'm in love all over and I love every moment of this feeling. Love still wins!

This man was everything I needed; we all seem to want what's not right for us and what's right for us we don't want. I dreamed of a light-skin brother around 5'10" to 6'3", 180 pounds, pretty feet and of course the 3 Cs; Crib, Car and Career. I got all of that except my man of my dreams was dark-skin.

I couldn't complain at all and let the racist stigma go of not dating a dark-skin brother. I stated in "How It All Happened" Bob my molester, my two second cousins, Antonio "Coop" Davis, the guy who put the gun to my head and Bernard my rapist, were all dark-skin however this brother was just right. As the axis wheel turned it was my luck not to run into another Leo after all, a relationship with a Leo hasn't worked for the last three times. I never came in contact with a Virgo before I was anxious to see if we meshed.

Picture it: Atlanta, July 13, 2015, it Thursday a mild summer day we both were in Kroger in the vegetable section, there stood this tall brother about 5'11", 180 pounds solid, looking good and smelling right. As I walked up he was standing by the green peppers looking very confused and frustrated. I approached him glancing up and down pretending to look for green peppers. Soon we both stood there looking confused and frustrated.

Kroger sells the pack of peppers with three in the bag; it comes with a red, orange and green pepper. I decided to take the green pepper from the bag out. I opened two bags gave him one and I kept the other, he thanked me and we went our separate ways. Not even a minute later we met up again in the gravy aisle and we both started laughing while we picked our gravy. I sparked up the conversation believing he was straight but I have plenty of straight friends so that wasn't a problem.

I said, "You must be cooking pepper steak!"
He replied, "Yep!"
I said, "Ironic, great minds think alike, bro." We laughed again.
He then asked, "Do you smoke weed?"
"I sure do," I replied.

He then told me to take down his number I put his number in my phone calling his phone and told him to lock me in under

Samuel. He said, "Cool, I'm Clinton, bro." We shook hands and walked away. I walked away smiling. I realized I just gave a total stranger my government name. I generally don't do that, especially with men. I always say my name is Trey. I felt a different spirit with him.

About two hours later, Clinton called and asked if I wanted to come over and smoke. Of course, I said yes. There are two things I don't turn down — free food and free weed! He texted his address and I was on the way. He lived 33 minutes away. I was hesitant at first because I didn't feel like the drive, but I went because I said I was coming.

I pulled into his driveway after an hour — traffic was horrible. I pulled behind a new black car in his driveway. I approached the door and heard dogs barking and coming to the door. There were two dogs standing at the screened door, barking and jumping up trying to get me. **LOL** They were so cute; one was white and the other was brown.

Clinton yelled for them to get back and let me in. The dogs began wagging their tails and jumping up and down as if they were glad to see me, then charged me and started jumping on my legs. Clinton yelled, "Brooklyn, Lacey, get down!" I told him it was cool, although I hated dogs I acted like I didn't. **Side Stare** He said, "Welcome to *mi casa*, make yourself at home."

Nice! I thought to myself. Immediately it came to my mind that the brother has all 3 Cs: Crib, Car and he has to have a Career. Now, where is his damn girlfriend?!

Clinton fired up his blunt and we smoked and the conversation covered everything under the sun — from what we do for a living, where we were from, our friends and family, our likes and our dislikes, etc. Neither of us mentioned if we had a boyfriend or girlfriend; it didn't seem to matter.

He was mad cool and I loved it. He reminded me of all of the best of my straight home boys. There's an emotion that I have never felt before with any other men; it was a strong connection. I could tell the feeling was intense on both sides. He broke it by asking if I wanted a plate of pepper steak. *Not only does he have the 3 C's, and a cool conversation he could cook too!* I was screaming YYYAAASSSSS all over my body with all of my senses!

We hung out a couple of more times at his crib before I invited him over to my house. By this time, two months passed and it was September. School was just starting back. I graduated with my Associates degree and took the summer off before heading straight back to school seeking my Bachelor's degree.

I purchased a new batch of my books *Eyes Without A Face* and *How It All Happened*. They arrived right before Clinton came over, leaving five or six boxes of books in my living room. I'd opened a couple of boxes to make sure the count was correct, when Clinton knocked on the door. I let him in without putting the books up or closing the boxes. Although it had been two months, I didn't want to tell him I was gay. Yet, I felt if he wasn't going to be around, he didn't need to know.

I let Clinton in and he sat down. Of course his nosey ass asked what was in the boxes. I'd never told him I was an author! I couldn't withhold any information anymore, so without further ado, I passed him a book and didn't utter another word. He looked at the cover, and then flipped the book and read the back.

I watched his eyes grow bigger while he read the back of the book! He stood up and at that point I thought he was about to walk out the door. Instead, he reached out with his hand and said,

"Come here, man." He pulled me in and gave me a hug. Clinton said, "Man, I was about to tell you I am gay, too."

We both laughed and I said, "What a relief!"

Clinton asked questions about the books and I explained a little before I said, "You have to read them both."

He asked where the other book was and I told him in the other box. Then Clinton asked how much the books were. I told him and he bought two right then and there. He giving me a $50 bill and said keep the change! We talked a little more about the books and then we started talking about our past relationships.

* * * * *

It took those six months after getting to know him and paying attention to the love he showed for me before I decided to go further with him. We had been having casual sex at this point for four months, and he wanted a relationship since the very first time we made love. The way he looked at me, held me, touched me and treated me was kind of scary because it reminded me of Price, but he came with the 3 Cs so I wasn't worried about him using me. This was truly love, and it wasn't rushed. I was ready for a relationship but I wanted a light-skin brother. I wasn't open to dating him.

The reason I fell in love with Clinton was I had a car accident on December 22, 2015. It was exactly a week after my birthday and he took care of me the entire time. I put the saying "You know my cycle something good was followed by something bad" out of my mind and call it what it was; KARMA.

Karma came back and I needed Clinton because I was betraying him. I just spent December 18 with #26 right after I came back from New Orleans, and then the very next day I spent with Clinton doing the same things I done with #26.

They were both so romantic. #26 got a room downtown at the Westin all set up with candles and roses. It was just like the Valentine's Day we spent together in 2012. Ironically, Clinton would do the SAME EXACT THING at the SAME EXACT place! **Speechless** Every day is a fight with temptation with your flesh you have to not give in, always remember karma and what you can handle if it's done to you.

The New Year of 2016 approached, and Clinton asked again for a relationship for the umpteenth time. Surprisingly I obliged and said, "Let's go, Daddy." We made it official on January 13. Looking back, laughing at our very first disagreement was about Facebook he wanted to post a picture or video of us I said, "No!" right away! I didn't want anyone to know who I was dating. It's not that I was trying to keep him a secret, legally I was still married and trying to seek a divorce and I didn't want everyone in my relationship. I wanted to keep that part of me private.

I agreed to post a picture only because I truly love him and I wanted the world to know the feeling I was feeling. After I posted one picture, I couldn't stop. I ended up posting pictures back to back. After feeling my love for him flourish even more, I opened the door for everyone to see. I uploaded about 20 more pictures, videos and a flipagram. I saw nothing but love when I looked at him and felt feelings even stronger than Price gave me when we first started dating. I was really in love this time.

I wanted candid pictures taken of me because he likes the way I look. I wanted random text messages of only things we get and because he was thinking of me. I guess ultimately I wanted to be happy and in love. I got everything I wanted; my dark-skin stigma was slowly going away and all I could think was this dark-skin brother was winning!

I noticed after three failed relationships I was giving less of myself in this relationship. I stated in *How It All Happened* that my last two relationships were not bad. I was guarding my heart. This relationship seemed like a got damn fairy tale and I was taking precautions. I knew when I felt too loved I pushed back. I didn't want to take these same traits into this new relationship.

I prayed I wouldn't fall in love with a whore again. I prayed when I met someone GOD revealed their intentions and true character to me. I wanted an increased spirit of discernment going forward. Clinton broke up with his ex-boyfriend in May, two months before we met; they were together for five years. His ex was younger than him. He bought his ex a car and even helped him pay for school, only to come home one day from working a 12-hour shift to find the dude in their bed with another man. I would have died. I understand because I was once in his shoes.

Clinton is a mirror of me. While I was with Price, the way he treated and acted towards me scared the living shit out me. He was me. I could do no wrong in his eyes. I was perfect in every way to him. I thought for a time he was my karma from cheating on #26. Clinton and I made a pact in the very beginning: no arguing and never going to sleep angry at one another.

Talking to Clinton meant I would have to stop talking to #26 in that way, and anyone else for that matter. When #26 found out about Clinton from Instagram, he called me. I didn't answer because I didn't know what to say. I posted a picture of us and didn't even think about #26 being a follower on there. I didn't want to lose him as a friend but I knew he would not even want to be friends. #26 started sending me text messages. I didn't reply right away. I was lost as to what to say exactly.

Before long, #26 sent me a text message saying he saw I have a "new little boyfriend" and I went about it the wrong way. He went on to say, "Good luck with your relationship and please don't ever hit me up again!" I was hurt but I had moved on. I felt like I was waiting for someone to come around when they were ready and I was not with that. Furthermore, throughout our conversations, #26 couldn't let go of the fact I cheated on him in the past and made it his business to throw it in my face all the time.

I gained all the weight back I lost after the breakup with Price and the surgeries. I weighed a whopping 154 pounds — that was the exact weight I weighed when I first met Price. I thought about Gary for a moment, gaining my weight back. I was in a relationship with Gary after Price and I broke up. When Price and I got back together, I brought Gary into the relationship.

I had no problem dating Gary and he was dark-skinned like Clinton. Gary and Clinton had many similarities — they both were the same height and weight, protectors and cherished their mates, and most importantly they both just wanted me to be happy in every way possible.

* * * * *

Clinton and I drove down to Florida to drop the dogs off with his grandparents while we got settled. February came, and my lease was coming to an end. We decided it was best to continue my lease and he move in with me. I paid the cheaper rent and we thought it would be best to save some money before we moved into something bigger.

We both wanted to purchase a house and knew it would be better to have a large down payment so our mortgage would be cheaper. Clinton has two dogs, (Babies) Brooklyn and Lacey, and thought before we moved in together and out of his place to take the dogs to his grandparents in Florida while we got settled. I was really about to be in a relationship now.

This would be my first time meeting his grandparents. His grandmother was nice. I had the feeling his grandfather didn't like me though. We were all sitting in the living room and his grandparents went into another room in the house. It was the room behind me and the wall separated us. His grandmother called him to come to the room.

His grandparents started asking Clinton all type of questions, "You don't know this young man, and we have never heard of him, how old is he?" The ultimate was when his grandfather said, "How you know he's not trying to use you?"

Say what now? Who? What? Where? When? Not me! I was livid and had to keep my composure when they all came out the room.

Clinton's grandmother started asking me questions, "What do you do for a living? Do you have your own place? and a lot of other questions. When I got done telling her about my life, what I've been through, where I'm going and how I was going to get there, she stood up and said, "I thank GOD for bringing you into my grandson's life!" She gave me a nice tight hug and I thought to myself, *I bet you weren't expecting that!* **Side Stare**

I was not Clinton's ex. I understood where she was coming from. His grandfather wouldn't even shake my hand when we left, he just said good-bye as if that was going to be the last time he saw me.

We came back home and immediately began the process of moving. I told Clinton before we started putting his things in boxes that I didn't do manual labor. He ended up getting one of his friends to help him because I wasn't lifting shit! I didn't move myself into my apartment, and I wasn't about to move him either. I loved him but manual labor hurt!

After we were done moving in, we went back to get the babies two weeks later, we needed some alone time for us. I'd known his babies since I met him and they loved me. The trip going to pick up the babies was better. This time around, grandmother was happy to see me and that we were still together. I believe they didn't think we would last those two weeks. **Blank Stare** Sadly, the grandfather was the same with that dry ass "Hello and good-bye!"

We spent Easter at our place. Timothy came in town for the holiday and Diane, Miyasha, Kevin, Keisha, Victor, and Onsemious were all here. Some of us played spades and others watched a movie called *Brotherly Love*. I cooked greens, deviled eggs with shrimps on top, yams and dressing. Clinton cooked jerk chicken and baked chicken. Timothy cooked his famous baked macaroni and cheese, however this batch was dry as hell. **Shade** Keisha brought over a bottle of Ciroc, Onsemious brought weed, Miyasha brought over wine, and Diane brought Clinton and me an Easter basket.

It seemed as if the holidays were coming back to back. My bae went crazy on the grill for Memorial Day. He grilled hamburgers, hotdogs, and chicken, plus cooked baked beans, potato salad, and macaroni and cheese but forgot the desert. Miyasha ended up bringing Strawberry Crunch Cake.

All of my friends loved Clinton and he liked them. We all hung out and went to the clubs with each other all the time. Miyasha would come over for dinner sometimes, and Timothy still came in from out of town and stayed with us. He just had to call first; he didn't have a key to the added lock on the door! This was a huge difference from being with Price — I couldn't trust my circle, everyone was sleeping with my man. Now I didn't have to worry about it this time around!

Like every relationship, we've experienced our fair share of ups and downs. No relationship is perfect and everyone has problems but it's how you deal with the problems that either keep you going or make you stop. Sometimes, I would shut down when we had a disagreement. If I felt the conversation was taking a turn for the worse I shut down. Clinton talked me through that and explained that sometimes we have to agree to disagree.

At other times, I felt like he was too damn nice. He reminded me of Eddie Murphy's "Queen to be" in *Coming to America*. I would say, "Bae what do you want to eat?" Clinton would say in return, "Whatever you want to eat." Or I'd say, "Bae what you want to do today." He would say, "Whatever you want to do today." It used to drive me crazy because I was like that with Price.

I would stay in my phone some days and Clinton would have an attitude. I knew he was upset sometimes, but if he didn't say anything I stayed in my phone. After a while, he finally said something but he blew up in a polite way. I was shocked. I didn't know how to take it. In the time we have been together he has NEVER raised his voice at me.

Clinton and I learned to agree to disagree. We are not perfect — no relationship is. We have had one huge argument before and it made me tear up. Clinton told me he can't help it. I have never had real love and for someone to show me attention starting with my mother to Price. Clinton said he wanted to show me the world but I was not allowing him to because I wouldn't open up, and I would disrespect him at times when talking to him. He felt I was talking to him as if he were stupid or a child, which I did.

At times, I would flinch when he touched me. I guess I would think of Price hitting me or picture him sleeping with my friends. I had to come to the realization that he was not Price. Clinton is nothing like Price. He's the total opposite. Sometimes when someone is being too nice we don't know how to take it. I learned to not be afraid to love again because not all people are like my ex.

I loved the things we did together. Clinton gave me a sense of security, stability, warmth and companionship, and I trusted him completely. Some people thought we were brothers because we started to look alike after being together and going almost everywhere together like we were Siamese twins attached at the hip. We went to the Drive-in every Friday — Bae is a movie fanatic. We attended a Super bowl party where Beyoncé was performing for the half time show **Funny Moment** my gay friends called it a "Beyoncé Concert."

When we went shopping. It would be funny as our interaction with each other would have people stopping in their tracks and looking at us. We would go to the mall and Clinton would say, "I don't like that it's too tight or pull your pants up you're showing your ass!" I would try and get him out of the habit of buying solid colors — he has so many red, blue and black clothes that it's insane. I wanted him to switch up, so he would let me pick out his clothes for the most part.

We went to the clubs together and I went with just my friends a couple of times. His friend Tristan reminds me of myself; he's very outgoing, fun to be around and classy. Clinton's other friend Adam, a Caucasian man, is laid back. He reminds me of TaQuan, he's Clinton's mentor. When I first learned that, it made me smile because we all need a mentor. We all need someone who can educate and inspire us to do better and be better.

It had almost been a year since I met Clinton at this point, we met July 13, 2015 and it was now May 2016. Being together almost a year is like being together for five years in the "Gay world." Now it was time to meet his mother, siblings, and some of his other family members…

CHAPTER 2

MIAMI WITH THE BESTIE

Oh life has had so much to offer, I never thought I would be actually living in my truth at this time. I was about to turn 36 years old and headed out of town to Miami with my bestie Timothy. It was the weekend of December 11, 2014. I've known Timothy at this point for five years. He's my partner in crime, human diary, little/ big brother, Brista (Brother/Sista), motha (Gay life), my right hand and my best fran — he is everything a best friend should be and the true definition of it.

*****

Timothy couldn't sleep the night before our trip and kept calling me. Honestly, I couldn't sleep either. He had to be at work the next morning and then had to turn around and drive four hours to Atlanta. We were leaving soon as he touched down to make the 10 drive down to Miami. Timothy lived in South Carolina and we both were excited to go on the trip. Neither of us has ever been to Miami. He wanted to take me to Miami for everything I went through in the years of 2013 and 2014.

Why Did We Meet? — It Wasn't' By Choice

The past couple years have been devastating with a total of seven surgeries, four in my mouth alone, my mom and I were not speaking, I attempted suicide and was admitted into a psychiatric hospital for nine days, and the biggest thing was I fell out with a few friends (Angela, Kevin and Quinton whom we are all friends with now). My bestie prepared a whole "Paid in full" vacation. Ya'll know I was game — hello and let's go!

The next day, Timothy got off work at 5 p.m. and hit the road to meet up with me here in Atlanta. He had to drive through Georgia to get to Miami anyway. He arrived at my house at 9 p.m. and we loaded my car, arranged our music, got gas, Red Bulls and 5-Hour Energy drinks and hit the road. I started off driving because he just drove four hours. By 10 p.m., we were on the road headed straight for the MIA!

We sang up and down the highway, the two us together driving was great — we were both road warriors. I had been driving from Minnesota to Chicago/Gary, from Minnesota to Dallas, Texas then from Dallas to Cali, Cali back to Dallas and Dallas to Atlanta. Timothy had been driving from Atlanta to Minnesota, Minnesota to North Carolina, then from North Carolina to South Carolina, with all the Atlanta trips in between. Splitting the hours up was great. We never got too tired to drive and no one was ever behind the wheel too long.

We arrived at the hotel in Miami right before 9 a.m. on Friday. Miami morning traffic was horrible. We could have arrived an hour earlier but we were stuck in traffic. Once we got to the hotel, we checked in. We were staying at the Court Yard by Marriott, a very nice hotel and Timothy received a good discount from his job. After getting in the room on the top floor of the fifteen-story building, we picked beds and crashed from the Red Bulls and 5-Hour Energy drinks.

I set my alarm clock for noon and shortly after falling asleep we were right back up. I showered first, while Timothy ironed his outfit. Then Timothy showered, and I ironed my outfit. The weather was the bomb — it was 80 something degrees and wasn't hot. Coming out of the hotel we were ready for our photo shoot outside. Every time we stepped out of the hotel, we took pictures and then we were ready to hit the scene. We drove around our hotel area to get a feel of where we were. We didn't see anything but Mexican this and Mexican that, shortly after we realized we were staying in the Mexican area. It wasn't bad it's just the majority of everything was written in Spanish from the stores to the restaurants — everything was in Spanish.

We left our hotel area and headed for the beach. We wanted to be around *our* people. Well, we really just wanted to be around some fine men — *hello!* On our way to the beach, we got lost on the turnpike. The turnpike wasn't expensive but it charged every time you entered. At some tolls we paid, and at others it charged my license tag on my car and the bill would come in the mail later. I think we rode through the turnpike about 100 times before the trip was actually over.

Finally we made it to a restaurant in downtown Miami. I wanted something Mexican and we were starving. Finding a parking spot in the garage took forever. Then we walked to this Mexican place we'd goggled it. It was an authentic Mexican restaurant and they had just about everything on the menu from Mexican tacos to tostados to enchiladas. We ordered our food and drinks — I ordered chicken tacos and Timothy ordered steak tacos.

I wanted steak tacos badly but my braces prevented me from enjoying that kind of meal. Wearing those braces was annoying and eating steak or chewy meats was time-consuming and hard to get out of my braces. While waiting for our food, we had drinks and shots. By the time the food came, I was drunk. I did a video with our waitress — I was feeling myself. I was going to do a video regardless!

We left the restaurant, went sightseeing by the beach, and drove around and looked at all the ships at the dock and out at sea. It was amazing to see a cruise ship up close — they are huge. The condos on the water were immaculate. They were tall and looked as if the buildings were made of glass, so much glass. The only thing I didn't like about Miami was the damn traffic.

It was close to 8 p.m. and we had only driven around the town and were stuck in traffic most of the time. We decided to grab a quick bite to eat and head back to the hotel to change clothes and go out to the club. We figured we should live in the night and head back to our hotel because of traffic.

Traffic was bad and backed up, and Timothy and I had to use the bathroom something fierce. We rode the emergency shoulder on the highway to exit off. When we finally got off, we couldn't find a restaurant, gas station or store to save our lives. We ended up at some kind of hotel/motel thing and used the bathroom there. Upon leaving, the GPS said 20 minutes at first to get back to our hotel, but it actually took us an hour and 20 minutes.

Once back at the hotel, we changed clothes and headed right back out the door to the club to turn up. It was my Birthday weekend bitches, wasn't any traffic about to stop us!

* * * * *

What a night we had, chile we partied at the club in downtown Miami until three-something in the morning. We didn't make it back to the hotel until after 5 a.m. We'd stopped to get something to eat at Denny's, the only place open by our hotel. We met a few people who treated us to drinks all night — men were always buying us drinks when we went out. **Smiling Hard** As soon as we got in our room we were out cold!

Timothy and I woke up after 2 p.m. on Saturday, and were really beat from the drive, the Red Bulls, and 5-Hour Energy drinks combined with the alcohol from the previous night. We were now well revived and ready to let Miami have it today. We were not heading back home until Sunday afternoon, so we knew we had to go hard and leave our names on the city that day. Timothy's friend called him after seeing he was in town from Facebook.

Timothy's friend lived in Miami but was from South Carolina where they went to school with each other. His friend was actually still in Las Vegas working but was going to be home in Miami later that night and told Timothy to stop by. After we were dressed, we were going to head to the strip once again. The weather was amazing at 80-something degrees.

Before we made it to the strip we looked for Biscayne Bay Blvd. for the "Golden Girls" home. We never found it but it was fun looking for it. **Blank Stare** We did find the mall and shopped until we were about to drop, but then we were finally off to the strip.

The strip was a place I will never forget — it was long, full of people and lots of things to see. There were many clubs, restaurants, nice cars riding up and down, and MEN, MEN, MEN and even more MEN! Men of all colors and all kinds of sexy bodies were up and down the strip. My neck broke a few times because every time a fine man walked past, I snapped my neck to look over.

There were many gay people due to all the many gay clubs. We stopped at one of the clubs while walking the strip but it wasn't our cup of tea. The club was more like a rave and we were not into that, however we were on Ocean Drive in South Beach getting our got damn life!

We sat down and ate at a steak restaurant outside on the patio of the building because the weather felt so good. The entrées were kind of expensive. Timothy told me to quit looking at prices. Shit, he only had to tell me once. I ordered a steak, garlic mashed potatoes, and asparagus. Fuck my braces today, I was about to eat! I could hardly eat while looking at all the gorgeous men of every race and nationality surrounding me: Black, White, Puerto Rican, Mexican, Cuban, Jamaican, and Spanish to Malottos — everybody was fine!

After eating, we decided to walk across the street to the beach and it was packed. People were out playing volleyball, skating, roller blading, singing, playing instruments, walking around and swimming in the water. The beach was cooler but I still took my shirt off to get a few pictures. I didn't get in the water because I still couldn't swim.

We were about to leave the beach and walk up the strip on Ocean Drive when I decided to check to see if my grades were posted. I know it was my birthday weekend and I was supposed to be relaxing and having a good time but I needed to know what my grades were.

The semester ended and our grades were to be posted on the school website before the 15th of the month. Sure enough, the grades were posted. I earned three Bs and one C, missing the honor role by one point, leaving me happy but pissed at the same time. I'd worked my ass off and I wanted to make the honor roll badly. I only had one semester to go until graduation. I was about to celebrate even harder now that I knew I passed all my classes.

At that moment, people started calling my phone. My birthday was on a Monday the 15th and everyone knew I was in Miami from my Facebook post. I was getting even more excited and I was tipsy, too. I wasn't drunk but I was feeling myself for sure. After walking the strip twice up and twice down then back to the car we decided to drive it. We drove up and down the strip about 15 times, screaming Beyoncé from the top of our lungs until we were hoarse. We did so many videos my phone said the storage was full.

Timothy's friend called during our last tour and we made our last appearance on the strip with the panoramic sunroof open, all the windows down, and the radio full blast as we were singing like we were in concert. We made our exit to Timothy's friend's house; he lived less than ten minutes from the strip in a condo.

When we pulled up, he was outside waiting for us on the sidewalk. He and Timothy embraced as Timothy introduced us. Timothy said, "Maine this is Sam, Sam this is Maine." Maine was my complexion and height. He was muscular, weighing around 180 or 190 pounds. He was solid with nice nipples peeking through his shirt, a country accent, and glasses; he was attractive.

Maine invited us to his place since he had friends over. We entered and immediately were met by two other gentlemen — Ken and I can't remember the other guy's name. Ken was a sexy redbone mixed with black and white and about 210 pounds, the other guy was a skinny queen and we paid her no attention at all!

We all sat down and they offered us drinks. Maine stated they were celebrating for his birthday weekend and Timothy yelled, "That's right — it is your birthday weekend!" I told him it's mine too! Maine asked when my birthday was and I replied, "December 15 and yours?"

Maine said, "December 11. Sagittarius, baby boy." Maine was flirting for sure.

We all sat down and drank our drinks and watched *Hangover II*. I sat next to Timothy, Maine sat at my feet, the skinny queen sat on the other side of Timothy and Ken sat across from all of us. We laughed and conversed with each other while drinking and eating potato chips. Meanwhile, Maine was rubbing my feet and we were smiling and flirting without using words, just body language.

I texted Timothy and asked, "Do you like or have you ever had anything going on with Maine?

Timothy replied and said, "NO" in bold letters. "We're strictly friends. I'm interested in Ken!"

"That's what's up" I texted back.

Timothy and I made a pact in the beginning of our friendship that we would never go behind each other or have relations with someone the other person had already had relations with. Our friendship was deep and no man would ever come between us — there was too much dick out here for that!

Time passed, Timothy and I talked Maine into going to the club. He wanted to sit home and get wasted but we weren't having that. We wanted to go out, plus we didn't live there. We heard a club called Club Boi was going to be popping.

Maine agreed to go out with us, so we left to go change clothes. We weren't even ready before Maine called and said to meet them at "Club Boi. They were about to head out. Timothy and I put some pep in our step and sped up our process of getting ready. We left the hotel and headed to the club. The club wasn't even twenty minutes away and when we pulled up the parking lot was jam-packed. We had to park at the back of the club because all the parking spaces were taken.

Maine and his crew were waiting for us at the door. We walked up they all hugged us and we proceeded to go in. I pulled out my ID and money after I was searched. Maine said, "I got him," and I was like *YYYAAASSSSSS* in my mind.

We went in and went straight to the bar. Maine bought the first round of drinks Timothy bought the second round, and the skinny queen bought the third — we were cool at this point I think he said his name was like Joe or something. Maine bought the rest of the drinks, and before long I was off to the dance floor.

Timothy's "friend" he met Friday called him and he left us, asking if I was okay. Maine said I was before I could speak up. Maine told Timothy he would make sure I got back to the hotel before it was time for us to check out. Timothy left and we followed behind him.

We went back to Maine's house and when Ken and ole boy got out, Maine asked did I want to go back to the hotel. He said he would spend the night with me. I obliged and he said, "But you have to drive." He was white boy wasted and I was tipsy but I wasn't drunk. I slowed down drinking after Timothy left.

Maine slept the entire ride to the hotel. I used the GPS on my phone to get us back to the hotel. I didn't know how to use the GPS in his car. Maine drove a 2014 Nissan Maxima and it rode very smooth. We arrived at the hotel and went straight to the room, stripped and laid in the bed. Maine held me the entire night very tight. He kissed on my back and neck on and off while we laid there. Early that morning, Timothy came back to the room. He couldn't get in right away because Maine put the latch on the door.

Timothy came in smiling and asking how my night went. I said, "Chile, please. How was your night?!" We laughed and started the process of getting ready. Timothy showered while we laid there and fooled around. When we heard the water turn off, we stopped and Maine got dressed while I threw on some shorts.

Timothy had to be at work Monday morning at 8 a.m. We needed to make sure to stick to the schedule since there was a 10-hour drive ahead of us and Timothy had an additional four hours to get back to his house. We were both ready, so Maine got up and we cuddled and kissed. He made me promise to keep in touch before we all walked out the door. Timothy and I didn't leave without taking our soft sets of hotel towels and without calling room service to get extra!

* * * * *

#26 and Clinton were the best way I ended my birthday celebration…

CHAPTER 3

GRADUATION AND BOOK RELEASE PARTY

Of course no one other than my bestie would be the one to plan my Graduation and Book Release party. It was set for May 9, 2015, so Timothy came in town Wednesday to wrap up the shopping. He had been here every weekend the month of April to ensure this went smoothly. I was still in school and I was stressing because I thought I was going to fail my History class. I found out nine weeks before graduation I had to take a History class because I didn't graduate from High School in the state of Georgia and it was a requirement for graduation bastards!

We had been planning this party for months and it was finally about to happen. Timothy was paying for the DJ, Tika my home girl from Gary High School and the hood was paying for my cake, Timothy's aunt was making the food and I was covering everything else from the venue, tables, chairs, food, to the decorations.

My guest list was for 75 people. I didn't want anything too big, just close friends and family. We had to get everything from plates, cups, napkins, tablecloths, signage, forks, knives, spoons, liquor, ice, coolers, food trays, the food burners, candles, podium, microphone, red carpet, and a TV projector. I still laugh to myself about how Timothy and I argued over the little things.

For instance, I wanted to get plastic red cups because they were cheaper Timothy wanted to get champagne glasses because they were classier. I didn't care about the classy cups, I was being cheap damn it! Those red cups were $6.34 and there were 100 of them. Wal-Mart didn't have the champagne glasses and I knew they were going to be expensive. Timothy said, "We are not having the party in the ghetto, so we are not buying them ghetto ass red cups!"

I said, "Chile, please, I was raised in the projects, ain't nothing wrong with them damn red cups!"

I didn't buy them. He was right, this celebration was going to be nothing but classy and he was going to make sure of that!

* * * * *

Timothy was in charge of sending out the invitations. I was in charge of getting everyone's addresses. Timothy and I made an event on Facebook to notify everyone that invitations were coming and we needed addresses so people could RSVP. It was getting hard, trying to keep track of those who were coming and calling to RSVP rather than sending the invite card back to us.

I was getting frustrated. Every week I was having a quiz or exam I was constantly studying I felt burnt out. I only had three classes my last semester but they were all hard. My last three classes were Principles of Accounting, Principles of Microeconomics and United States History 1. I was struggling in two of my classes and the History class just overwhelmed me.

The History class was an eight-week mini semester course. It was three hours and 20 minutes long and nothing short of a lecture class. I was pissed I had to take the class. It just added stress to my life, but surprisingly I loved History class! I learned things I never knew. The "Slave Trade" blew my mind and hurt me to the core. So many of my people with melanin skin were taken from their land and brought over to the 13 colonies and made slaves.

It was hard to digest the information without tearing up, even harder knowing that our people turned on one another for the slave masters. We still see this today with us turning on one another from hatred and jealousy. I couldn't believe what they did to my people and to see us doing the exact same thing to each other daily it's pathetic.

I learned about the "Slave Patrol" too. The Slave Patrol is somewhat like our police today: profiling, illegal searches, beatings, the prisons and the judicial system are all works of the slave patrol. I learned a system that wasn't made for us can never protect us. I learned about Andrew Jackson and the "Indian Removal Act of 1830." I also learned about the genocide with the "Trail of Tears in 1838."

Graduation was quickly approaching. I found myself sad and it seemed hard to shake it. I found myself crying and praying throughout the days leading up to graduation. I was sad for a couple of reasons — my best straight friend Onsemious wasn't graduating, he became so wrapped up in girls he was skipping school to be with them. He got arrested for an old charge and was locked up for a little over a month. He needed six classes total to graduate and that was not going to happen.

My mom wasn't coming. We were still not talking and I didn't even know what state my mother lived in. She'd moved from

Minnesota to Indianapolis to Memphis and then to Arkansas. She was running. She kept saying the government was after her — the government had placed a "Blue beam in her ear and was tracking her!" I been saying my mother needed help and was having a nervous breakdown. I think it's even deeper and she may be either bipolar, schizophrenic or both.

I prayed my mother would get help. She was angry and I wanted to have her committed but I had to let my mother go. After all, she'd let me go a long time before. I love my mother with all my heart. It hurt me to the core to not have my mother's love. It really bothered me that all my gay friends had their mothers in their corners and I didn't.

I didn't invite my mom's side of the family. I wanted to connect with my dad's side. I knew if my mother's side of the family filled the room I would have gravitated towards them since I know them well. My dad's side of the family I was really getting to know it had only been a few years I been around them. I wanted to ensure our bond was strong. I wanted them to know everything about me. I didn't have to hide anything; I wanted them to know Samuel! I did invite my brother, sister, and my cousins Nina and Felicia. I knew they couldn't come but I sent out the invitations anyway.

My sister's husband was sick; he had a stroke. My brother was in-between homes and he was pussy struck and so stuck on pussy he didn't know if he was going left or coming right. There would have had to be a pussy in his face in route to Georgia to make him come. Felicia's daughter, Bre, was graduating and it was her prom weekend on the same weekend that I was graduating. My favorite cousin/sister Nina just relocated to Michigan City from Minnesota and I knew that was out the question. I was cool. I knew why they all couldn't come. They all were there with me in spirit and all of them sent a gift except my brother.

It was three days before graduation and I was ready to turn up. I was so elated I was finally graduating from college with my Associates Degree in Business Administration. This was another accomplishment to add to my list. I'd come a long way from being kicked out of college in Minnesota and having to be paid for sex to pay for my education. YYAAAASSSSSSSS!

In addition, I completed my second book, *How It All Happened*, which was a sequel to *Eyes Without A Face! How It All Happened* allowed people to see how things happened and the depth of many situations. It tells the start of my growth, how I was starting the process of forgiving and how I was going to make a change one day with help or by doing it myself! I was accomplishing everything I set out to do on my vision board. I wasn't anywhere near done chasing my dreams and fulfilling my goals. I was on a mission.

Eli and I hooked up later in the day on May 5. He was a classmate I met in college, and he was cool. Eli was from Oklahoma and full-blooded Indian. I always had a melting pot of friends. I've learned in order to expand your horizons you should have a mixed culture of friends. Eli was going to school to become a doctor and he still had another year to complete his degree.

Eli and I went out to eat first at the Cheesecake Bistro in Atlantic Station. I had been craving salmon and we decided to go there. I ordered the baked crusted salmon entrée along with garlic mashed potatoes and the vegetable medley. It was scrumptious. Eli ordered the shrimp fettuccine. Our waitress gave us a discount on our meal because I was graduating. She was eavesdropping on our conversation while she was walking around taking orders either that or I was just happy as hell and loud and kept saying I was graduating!

When we were done eating, we paid and left to walk around Atlantic Station. We went in and out of stores, along with some good old window-shopping. I did end up buying some gym shoes. I'm such a shoe whore. We left Atlantic Station and headed to Piedmont Park. It was nice outside and the sun was still up. We walked around the park twice, did a couple of videos and took pictures as the sun began to set. Neither of us was ready to turn in and decided to go to Blake's on the Park across the street from Piedmont Park.

We walked through the door and I knew it was going to be a long night. There were many fine men and we owned the room — when we stepped through the door, all eyes were truly on us. Eli was this tall strappy redbone American Indian and I was just little ole me, of course. Before long, people were buying us so many drinks I had to start refusing them. I was driving. Eli took all the drinks I turned down and never got drunk! The night turned into day as we left the club and I dropped Eli off. My girl Molly was flying in town from Minnesota early in the morning and I had to pick her up from the airport.

I was up and ready to head to the airport by 10 a.m. Molly's flight was landing at 10:30 a.m. and she was staying until Sunday. Molly was initially Price, my ex-husband's friend. She was one of his very close friends. She told me before I knew he was cheating and I didn't believe her, maybe I didn't *want* to believe her. It's funny how life is. Molly was now one of my best friends and not friends with Price at all. Molly is my home girl, she's Caucasian and cool; she's a beautician and her hair is always laid!

When Molly came out of the airport, I was parked and standing on the curb. We embraced each other immediately. I hadn't seen her since last year in June when I went to Minnesota for my niece's graduation. We got in the car and headed back to my crib before stopping to get some weed.

I had some weed but Molly wanted her own sack. I took her to my "Weedman's" home and she bought a $100 worth. I said, "Bitch, are we smoking or are we smoking?" We both laughed and I pulled off. We headed up the street to my house so she could get settled and change clothes. Timothy was heading to Atlanta and arriving shortly.

Molly changed clothes and then she rolled a couple blunts and we hit the streets of ATL. Molly had never been here before, so I thought I would show her around. I didn't know the city like I knew Minneapolis but I knew some cool spots to see. I also had to pick up my cap and gown at the school.

Everyone that was graduating was fitted in April and our caps and gowns would be available the week of graduation. I received my cap and gown and I did a short video and posted it to Facebook. I was doing videos to mark every big event in my life. I was doing videos of me singing, I was just doing videos to be doing videos for when I died people so they can have something to look back on and see me.

As soon as Timothy arrived at my house, we all headed back out. I knew we were going to be in and out all weekend and I needed to grab the last of the minor things from Wal-Mart . We all headed there when Miyasha came over. Chile, when I tell you we had to run through Wal-Mart to catch the barbershop before the shop closed and get everything, we were running fast! Between Timothy, Molly, Miyasha and myself we got a total of 40 items and were in and out within 30 minutes! Miyasha had given me $50 in food stamps and that paid for all the food on my list for the party.

We made plans to go to Spondivits my favorite restaurant. I loved seafood and Spondivits was the shit. Our wait was an hour and 15 minutes! We sat our asses right outside on the benches in front of Spondivits with our drinks we ordered from the bar. It was a nice night and we enjoyed each other, catching up on time missed. Timothy and Molly met when Timothy lived in Minnesota. I loved the fact I comingled all my friends — straight, gay, men, women, black, white and American Indian.

Spondivits was definitely the place to be. It was a full house that night — I think it's a full house every night. Some customers got into it with the hostess and she wouldn't add their name to the list. Spondivits' rule is everyone in your party has to be present in order to add your group's name to the list, if not you have to wait until everyone arrives. We didn't have that problem since we all rode together. After the long wait, we were finally seated. I was not a fan of where they sat us but the wait was longer for another table. We were smack dead in the back next to the kitchen and the traffic by us was horrible.

Our waiter made light of the situation a little because he was fine a red bone with a body you would just want to grab and touch all over. He looked like he could fuck like a porn star and do it very good too — you know all porn stars can't fuck good! **Side Stare** I couldn't help but to stare at him — I mean I stared this man down! I had gotten a little beyond myself and told him how fine he was.

When he took our orders I said, "Hey, Cody. (That was his name.) I don't want to offend you and I apologize in advance, but you are gorgeous!"

He responded, "Thank you. I really 'preciate that." (Just about everyone here in ATL says 'preciate instead of appreciate.) Then this pretty motherfucker had the nerve to kind of smile and stare back with eye contact. I couldn't take him and turned my head. He was too fine and one of us was going to be in trouble and it wasn't going to be me.

The servers kept walking past and yelling out orders. I thought I'd turned into a damn waiter I heard so many orders placed for the cooks/ I said, "And that's going to have broccoli with it or fries?" I was kind of irritated but the alcohol kept that under control, and now I was on my second drink. I am a lightweight when it comes to alcohol; smoking weed is my thing.

Our food came out and I was ready to smash. I ordered the combo bucket. It comes with lobster, shrimp and King crab legs steamed in garlic butter and old bay seasoning. Molly ordered the fried salmon sandwich with fries, and Timothy ordered the fried combo — it came with fried shrimp, oysters and clams — and Miyasha had the same thing I did. We all ate from each other's plate. Every time the waiter came, I flirted with him. He was so damn fine, and he flirted back!

It was the day before graduation. Timothy had an appointment at the Honda dealership at 8 a.m. He was buying a new car for my graduation gift "for himself!" He initially was going to buy my car, but he decided he wanted to go "new." I understood with no problem. I would have gone "new" too.

Molly and I were smoking and lounging while he was out. I was still busy making calls and last minute arrangements. Timothy got back to the house around 6 p.m., along with his brand new fully loaded 2015 Honda Accord. He called his new car "Cookie Lyon!"

Miyasha came over to take some of my burden off and took over the phone calls. She made the last minute arrangements I almost forgotten about. I was glad my girl had a copy of my "To Do List!"

I had to go to the school for practice for graduation. I raced up to the campus and came back right after rehearsal. When I returned, we all piled up in "Cookie Lyon" and went shopping at Atlantic Station. There were so many stores to choose from but I only needed dress clothes. I purchased my outfit for my party online and from a T-Shirt designer. I was going to be the shit when I stepped through the door at my party.

After we returned home, we ran into this fine chocolate boy who was outside in my parking lot walking a dog. I'd seen him a few times before. (You will read about "My Neighbor" later!)

My stepsister Greta (my sister because we don't say step) called to let me know they arrived in Georgia. My dad, step mom (mom), niece and nephew had driven up from Gary, Indiana. I blocked off hotel rooms for everyone, but my Aunts Ann and Katt, cousins Tory, Demetri (Tory's brother) and Tory's kids blocked off rooms at the W Hotel in Buckhead for all of them. My Aunt Ann and her children came from Alabama and Dallas, and my Aunt Katt came from South Carolina. Aunt Ann and Aunt Katt are my dad's sisters. They were all going to meet me at the graduation the next morning since they still had a two-hour drive ahead of them.

*****

GRADUATION DAY MAY 9, 2015

I MADE IT! I MADE IT! GOD never left me. He'd been there the entire time. I know He had to be, since there were times I didn't think I would make it to graduation day. I defied all the odds. I had been sick, had multiple surgeries, tried to commit suicide and at times dropped a class or two. I was in a zone no one could ruin. I was graduating from College with my Associates Degree in Business Administration! Boy, you betta work!

I woke up before my alarm clock that morning. I had to be at the college before 8:30 a.m. for practice and pictures. My sister called me to ensure they knew where they were going. I'd sent the address the night before. Timothy took the phone and told me to hurry up and get ready while he gave directions and told them they should meet up so they could all sit together. They exchanged numbers and Timothy gave me back my phone before my sister said, "Congratulations, little brother!"

I walked out the door and got in my car. I was dressed down in my wife-beater and black slacks, black socks, black dress shoes. My lime green tie and white long sleeved dress shirt were on a hanger. I wanted to make sure I was seen before I put on my cap and gown and my shirt wouldn't be wrinkled.

Soon as I pulled off, I turned the radio on and Jennifer Hudson's song "I Got This" came on. Instantly I started crying. I couldn't help but think of my mother. I thought about everything I went through between us within my life. Oh, how I wished my mother was there to see me walk across the stage. I wanted her to know I wasn't stupid and I wanted to make her proud. I wanted to feel like I felt when I graduated from high school with her standing there taking pictures supporting me. I wish my mother loved me.

I had mixed feelings. I felt so big on one hand and very small on the other. I was so grateful to have my biological dad at my graduation; he'd missed about every important event of my life and now was his chance to see me do something great. In addition, my mom (stepmom), sister, niece, nephew, aunts and cousins all from my dad's side were here along with my friends. I felt GOD thought best at what I needed and I was fine with that.

Once I arrived at the school I saw many familiar faces, just about everyone I had classes with were graduating and the atmosphere was incredible with positive energy. I took pictures with lots of classmates and school pictures with the photographer there. They served breakfast before we started to line up, I passed I was not about to go through the issues of getting food out of my braces but my damn stomach was growing. Our names were on the back of the chairs there were 386 of us graduating this year from "Atlanta Metropolitan State College." That was the largest class ever!

When we were all seated a lady from administration gave us the directions on what to do again and told all of us "Congratulations." The President of the school said a little something before congratulating us also, and then we all stood up and began walking out the door headed to the gymnasium for the actual graduation. I did a short video walking to the gymnasium and posted it to Facebook I wanted to cry so badly. We walked into the gymnasium where the bleachers were all filled they had the over flow of people in an entire different building watching from projector screens. The rush I had running through me was intense I could not hold back my tears as we all waved at the crowds and they cheered us on.

Everyone was clapping and screaming out the people's names they knew, I loved it! I walked to my seat following the line I saw my dad and everyone else all sitting together holding balloons, taking pictures and screaming my name, the tears just flowed from the love. I felt everyone was here to support me!

The President of the school and other high profile people gave speeches. The Salutatorian and our Valedictorian gave speeches as well. The lady from administration started calling our names in order depending on degrees. When your name was called you walked on stage, receive your degree, walk toward the President of the school, turn and take a picture then exit the stage all while you're on a projector screen for the people who could not fit in the gymnasium.

When my name was called I had to man up and stop crying, this was my time to shine I was finally getting my degree. I started walking toward the stage and I felt people taking pictures from everywhere. My straight crew was on the opposite side of my dad's people. I received my degree, shook the President's hand, took my picture and exited the stage. I was walking toward my seat and a couple of professors called me over and gave me hugs, the entire faculty sat to the left of us. After we all received our degrees the President said something in closing and the crowd stood up and we exited the gymnasium. We all gathered outside and our families met us in the 90 degree weather we took pictures and hurried to the cars to get out of the heat.

My dad and his family, Timothy, Molly and I followed each other to Golden Corral. My sister paid for me and gave me $300 before we even sat down, our relationship had come so far it's not that I didn't like my sister I was jealous, I felt she had the chance of growing up with my dad and I didn't. Greta became a best friend we talked all the time and gave each other advice. After we all ate my dad and all of them went shopping and we headed home, my friend Marilyn's flight was landing in the next hour.

Timothy and I went to the airport to pick up Marilyn in "Cookie Lyon." We were going everywhere in "Cookie Lyon" there was no need to take "Sebastian" anywhere unless I absolutely had to. Marilyn flew in from New Orleans I'd known her since I was 21 years old. I worked at the Credit Union and she was a member there, she was also my home girl and like a mother figure. I always kept in close contact with her throughout the entire time since I left Minnesota. We all went back to the house but not before stopping at my "Weedman's" house. Molly gave me another $100 and Marilyn wanted a $50 sack. Chile when I say we smoked, we smoked and I didn't have to pay for weed the entire weekend and smoked like a chimney.

That night Molly, Marilyn, Miyasha, and Timothy stayed with me, we all chilled and talked the night away. The next day was going to be big I hadn't had a party like this since my wedding in 2008 on the yacht. This wasn't going to be that size but it felt like that magnitude because I was celebrating my graduation and the book release of my second book "How It All Happened!" We all woke up and Timothy and I cooked breakfast. We had to get a move on everything; we had to head over to Miyasha's because the party was being held in her club house at her apartment complex. The venue was beautiful with cherry wood cabinets in the kitchen, black appliances, a fire place, a huge open floor plan and a pool outside, it was simply breathtaking.

The place where I had rented the tables, chairs, podium, microphone, and projector screen forgot the red carpet and I had to go pick it up along with Rich the camera man and my classmate. Rich did my photo shoot for the cover of my second book "How It All Happened." Miyasha picked up the cake and chicken, Timothy had to meet his aunt to pick up the food, Molly and Marilyn put up all the decorations and organized the tables. When the work was all done we had to get ready. Lawd a house full of women with only 2 bathrooms was doing the most. Timothy went first so he could be at the venue to let people in who would be arriving soon.

Finally Molly and I were ready and headed over to the venue, the colors on the invitation said it was a black and white affair I wore red, black and white I wanted to stand out, hey it was my party! My shirt was red, and white with my first book "Eyes Without A Face" cover on the front and my second book "How It All Happened" cover on the back, my shorts were white I purchased them online they were knickerbockers they had black and white plaid on the end them, my shoes were white Airmax I had on a black leather NYC fitted cap along with a black metal link Michael Kors watch. I SLAYED!

Everyone was at the party when Molly and I walked through the door. They were standing in the entrance congratulating and clapping for me, I was in heaven I felt and received all the love and support. The red carpet was rolled out and everyone took pictures on it, my dad's sides were there, Moe, Timothy's best friend, came all the way from Virginia just for the day. Eli from school came with his friend. Will, Luciano's friend, came with his friend. Then Tiara my home girl I met while working at Macy's during Christmas one year was there. Shemia, my cousin Demetri baby mother, was there. Shemia and I built a relationship outside of my cousin.

Sharon came too, she was TaQuan and David's friend, my circle was complete all from networking. My friends Ron, Ebony, Robert, Jeanette, from my local post office came, they knew me so well I was constantly mailing off my books at their location. Vernetta and Cheri came, they were Kevin's friends from work, we had a bond too. Pearl and Moni came, they were my old neighbors from when I lived in Decatur and my girls. I had a room of about 75 people total and everyone brought cards and gifts I felt even more special when my straight homies Onsemious, Cody and Dutch came.

Onsemious was down because he didn't graduate but he said he had to support me. I loved him like he was my little brother. To top everything off my date Eric came. Eric was someone I had been having relations with for a couple of months and of course I wanted someone cute around my shoulder. Eric was very stable, once married to a woman and has an 18 year old daughter and he's a sergeant in the army. Eric was not relationship material I kept it what it was, just sex. I gave my speech and cried during most of it. I love my dad so much and it felt so good he was in my presence I could not stop crying while speaking of him. I thanked him so much for coming and bringing our family with him.

After the party was over we all hugged good-bye. My dad and the family were all leaving that morning headed back to Gary, Alabama, Dallas and South Carolina. I was thankful and blessed they all came, GOD knew best. The rest of us went to Bulldogs and partied like it was 1999. I was so damn drunk after the club. While taking pictures outside the club I was on Timothy's brand new car and scratched it! He was mad but he brushed it off, he knew I didn't mean it and I was drunk but he sure did curse me out. We left the club headed to the Waffle House before we headed back to my place. That will be a long week etched in my mind forever!

CHAPTER 4

MY PEACE

My peace of mind was the main thing I was concerning myself with even if it meant losing loved ones because of what I stood for so be it. No one else had to live with the things that happened to me and no one took care of me. With my peace of mind came my health, my surroundings and the people within my life. There were no exceptions and no one got a pass either, you are for me or in my eyes you were against me.

I was doing exactly what I said I was going to do which was live my life like it was golden I was living everyday if it were my last. I made sure to focus on my goals, love me, love those who loved me and see the world. I still made sure to try and not have any negativity within my life, no negative thoughts or feelings, and always tried to remain stress free my motto are pray more and worry less.

My health was great I was still Undetectable and my "T-cell" count was over 700 "Viral Load" 20. I didn't have to go to the doctor every 3 months anymore that was a huge relief I hated having to give all those tubes of blood every 3 months.

When I first found out I was positive I wanted to die. My ex-husband gave it to me he didn't tell me he tested positive until he found out 2 weeks after the fact. We had sex about every day from the date of his diagnosis. I should have known something wasn't right because we stopped having sex up until that point. However I remained hopeful and started taking the meds to ensure my HIV status wouldn't turn into AIDS. (If your T-cell count drops below 200 you are diagnosed with AIDS. There is no coming back to HIV status once you have the diagnosis of AIDS regardless if your T-cell count climbs back over 200)

I started to educate myself about the disease to ensure I had thorough knowledge of it. I went on a mission to inform others about it and how to deal with it. I learned I had to stay positive, keep negative people away because it causes stress. Stress takes your T-cell count down and makes your viral load go up. I had to eat right and exercise and most of all stay prayed up. I have HIV, HIV does not have me!

My braces were taken off January 21, 2016 and I was eating everything possible. I had been wearing braces since September 25, 2013 I wore them things for a whole 2 years 3 months and 27 days after the carjacking and seven surgeries total. Before long I didn't even have to wear a belt anymore with my pants or shorts I was getting fat.

I wasn't stressed and I say my mental state of mind was okay I still had some bad days but I never complained because I knew things could always be worse. I didn't have suicidal thoughts anymore and I was glad I didn't kill myself April 2014 when I attempted suicide. Having depression and anxiety was a lot at times. I really didn't care about anything then on the other hand I cared too much about everything. Having both was hell but I have it under control I was seeing my nutritionist and physiatrist faithfully once a week.

I found my coping skills to deal with the pain I endured unlike some people they don't seek help after horrific events happen to them and they live with the pain forever. My coping skills were writing, reading and singing. Writing is my strongest coping skill and I use it to the best of my advantage. I wrote just about everything down for some strange reason it made me feel good after I wrote something down. Singing was good I was able to scream while singing sometimes we have to scream. I would listen to a song and keep it on repeat until I knew the words by heart.

There were some things that made my spirit uneasy; the fact I didn't have my mother, brother and aunt in my life kind of bothered me but I didn't let it hurt me to the point I couldn't focus. I hadn't spoken to my mother since June 1 of 2014, 2 entire years. My Aunt Sheri still didn't talk to me, I stopped talking to my brother and my dad Robert was estranged.

I tried to sweep these issues away but they never went anywhere. Mother's Day, my mother's birthday, her parent's birthday, and holiday's, family functions, anything big within my life, anything going wrong, anything going right, or if I'm in pain, I always thought of my mother. So many things always reminded me of my mother. When I hurt for my mother I hurt badly. I was envious of my ex's because they all have great relationships with their mothers.

Mother's Day approaches every year this year I felt a bit different. I've always questioned my mother's actions and why she beat me after finding out her boyfriend molested me, not loving me because of my sexuality and because of my books I've written; "Eyes Without A Face" and "How It All Happened." I also understand why my mother gave my sister Teresa away to her aunt to be raised. By the negative comments I've seen on my Facebook thread regarding the men whom molested me, my mother had to think just like these same individuals; they either couldn't believe it, or it happened to them in their past. The part I'm having a hard time dealing with is I am her child, her baby boy.

My mother was given an ultimatum when she gave my sister away at 6 months old. She already had my brother, she wasn't finish with high school and my grandmother wanted to ensure my mother was capable of raising her children. With the promise of my mother finishing school and getting a job to support her now 2 children, her daughter would be given back. That didn't happen and my mother lost her child to her aunt. Today I forgive just like yesterday, the day before that, the year before that and the couple of years before that I understand. I will forever love my mother and I wish you a Happy Mother' Day In advance this year and every year going forward.

To anyone that doesn't have their mother in their life I understand your feelings and the pain associated with it. I want my mother to know she is one of the reasons why I wrote "Eyes Without A Face" and "How It All Happened." I want all mothers to know not loving and supporting your child or children hurts them more than you'll ever imagine. I want children to know if you do have your mother in your life to obey and cherish her. You can have a thousand daddies but you will only have 1 mother. I love you so much momma!

My brother Romie and I had words because he felt I shouldn't post anything on Facebook about the men who molested me which were all his friends. Every time I post anything of them he would call me and ask me to take it down, I never did! He felt I was being messy by posting anything about them, I felt it was foul that the men who molested me felt free to be able call him whenever they heard I posted something about them on Facebook. I felt he was wrong as fuck for still talking to these motherfuckers. Sadly I deleted and blocked my brother from Facebook. He still didn't understand why I post the things I post about "his friends" even after I've explained many times, "Ain't nobody got time for that!"

I sit back sometimes and think about my brother. Romie had really stepped up at first after my first book "Eyes Without A Face" came out and became the brother I really needed years ago. My brother started acting like a father instead of my brother and I loved it. I remembered a moment when Romie and I were young children; we used to play a game called "Knuckles." Romie would show me how to put my hands together like I was making a circle or a snow ball with the arch in my fingers and he would do it too.

Romie would show me how to play by thumping my knuckles. He would do it soft the first time then I would thump him. He would then say "Get ready, arch your knuckles up and hold your hands real tight!" I would do it and every time he would pop the shit out of my fingers, silly me I never learned. We use to wrestle, act like we were two of the three stooges (which our mom hated) and I used to play with his lips I had a bad habit as a child touching and rubbing on people's lips, he would bite my fingers to make me stop whenever I touched his.

I guess when I think about it I really didn't know my auntie so it shouldn't affect me that she didn't care for me. I think it was the support coming from someone with the title of "Auntie" this is my mother's sister my grandfather's daughter. Aunties and uncle's play an intricate role in raising children they are the next in line as role models. I loved all my aunties and they all loved me except for her. I guess because I missed my mother's love I felt I could receive it from my aunt. I understand my auntie was a Christian but so is my sister.

I hadn't talked to my daddy Robert in over a year every time I called his phone was disconnected. The last time he called me before I changed my number he said he lost his phone he was always losing his phone and getting new numbers. **Blank Stare** My daddy still couldn't admit he was a heroin addict I came to grips with it the last time I'd seen him when Timothy and I went to Minnesota. We stopped to see my dad he was looking so bad my dad use to be a heavy set guy and he was weighing just a little more than me when I weighed 135 pounds. I still can't get over the fact he asked me for money to buy drugs.

My dad did that every time I seen him I hate to see my dad be so far gone. Heroin completly took over his life; he looks like he didn't care about anything. I asked him if he wanted to go to rehab and he told me "People go to rehab when they have a drug problem and I don't have one!" As he said that I was standing there looking at someone who had a job, home, car, a little money and now doesn't have a pot to piss in. I was so irritated all I could do was hug him good-bye, tell him I loved him and also tell him we have to get some life insurance for you dad he laughed and said okay. I was serious!

Once I stop thinking about all of the madness I would think of the blessings I do have. I made up with my two cousins from Minnesota. I seen my girl cousin at our last "Edmond Family Reunion" in August of 2013. We spoke and talked about the issues and let it go. When I went to Minnesota for our Family Reunion with Timothy both my cousins were there they are my Uncle Kenny's children. We all talked, hugged, apologized and moved on we learned no matter what we are still cousins at the end of the day.

My sister Teresa and I grew even closer it felt good having a sister and especially one who loved me for me. I learned to deal with those moments I see pictures of her and think of our mother my sister looks like the spitting image of my mother and it was always bitter sweet. My nieces adored me and Teresa's oldest daughter Alexus look just like me Kayla the youngest looks like my brother Romie.

Teresa, my sister, is my mentor, advisor and motivator she is my praying sister and I definitely needed the prayers. I wished my sister and I lived closer to one another she lived on one end of the United States in California and I lived on the other end in Georgia. I missed my sister so much I can't help but think of how I feel. When I'm in her presence I sense of calming, I feel so lite like every burden has been lifted from me I feel extra loved.

The relationship I have with my grandmother is impeccable I love this lady more than I ever have in my life I can't help it I used to think she didn't love me. I learned it wasn't that she didn't love me, she didn't understand my "Life Style." I call my grandmother sometimes just to hear her voice and to tell her I love her. I often think back when I was a little kid she use to pick Troy and I up on Sundays and take us with her over to her mother's house for Sunday's dinner.

Some of her sisters would be over and a lot of my boy cousins would be outside in the front yard playing. I would be right in the house in the kitchen with the girls and women learning how to cook. I used to whip up the best cakes when I was little and I realized both my grandmothers taught me how to cook it wasn't just my dad Robert's mother Minnie.

My Father Samuel, Francine (mom) and my siblings were a blessing in disguise. All those years growing up I never knew my father would actually be playing the role of my dad being now my dad Robert was in a different state of mind. Here it is GOD blessed me with a mother because my mother wasn't in the picture. GOD had also given me more siblings to spread the love, with my father came a whole additional family.

It was crazy although my siblings on my dad's side are not his biological children we have a bond that feels like we are. My sister Greta reminded me so much of my sister Teresa she is also a praying sister that's heavy into the church. I felt deprived not growing up with her and my brothers, the look in Greta's eyes today brings tears to my eyes and she treats me like my sister Teresa treats me.

My brothers James and Phil are cool too they both are my brother's age; I am the baby of my siblings on both sides. I never really see them often their always working when I come to Gary. When I do see them it's like trying to play catch up. James and Phil respect me as their brother and nothing more, the way they love me is the way I want my brother Romie to love me.

I have a host of cousins, aunts and uncles, just like on my mom's side, I have favorite aunts on my father's side. My Aunt Ann is like a mother she reminded me of my Aunt Sylvia. Aunt Ann's children Demetri and Tori were my favorite cousins, my cousins Marcus and Marcellous felt like my brothers, like my cousins Troy and Demetrius on my mom side. It's insane how GOD blessed me when it came to my father coming back into my life.

From my mother I have five nieces, one1 nephew and two great grandnieces, from my father I have three nephews and two nieces. I have a total of four nephews, seven nieces, and two great nieces I felt old but good about it, I knew some people were not privileged to live as long as I have. My brother Romie's son, my nephew

DeAndre, is 23 years old and the oldest of them all and is incarcerated to this day. I haven't seen him since he was three years old.

My nephew DeAndre has two little girls whom I've yet to meet, Aniah is seven, and her little sister, Aliyanna, is four. Their mother Miriam is from Ixtapa, Zihuantanejo in the Mexican State of Guerrero. They were married on the same exact date as Price and I. The ironic part was they too separated my nephew wasn't ready like Price my nephew was too young and didn't understand how one should carry themselves when married.

My oldest niece on my dad side from my brother Phil is Kanessa 23 years old, goes to college and working. My brother Romie twins Tianna and Raonna are 20 years old and also in college and the Army Reserves. My sister Teresa daughter Alexus 18 years old and was next to graduate. My brother James's daughter Jayla is 14 and going to the ninth grade. My brother Romie's last child is little Zadie she's 13 years old going on 33 years old and going to the eighth grade. **LOL** Kayla my sister Teresa's daughter, Chris my brother Phil's son and James Jr., my brother James's son are all 12 years old and are going to the seventh grade. My sister Greta has the youngest baby boy little Lon and he's 3 years old.

They say everybody is not your friend and I strongly agree with that. I have some awesome friends though my true friends are very supportive. My friends are written throughout this book and within my other books *Eyes Without A Face* and *How It All Happened*.

My in laws were doing great. Keisha, Price's Aunt, still lived in Minnesota, I was happy for her and her two boys she was making a way out of no way coming from Chicago. She had been living in Minnesota for 3 years with no family and is doing great. Mary, Price's Mother, was also doing well. I hadn't spoken to her since I saw her last in June of 2014. I spoke to Keisha quite often she kept me up to date with how the family was doing.

My aunts and mom had talked about my Auntie Beverly since I was a child yet she'd never been around. Beverly is my mom's father's daughter she was his last child conceived after the divorce from my grandmother. She grew up in Gary and later moved to Arkansas. My mother and her siblings met Aunt Beverly when she was 15 years old.

Beverly was born after Aunt Teresa, I knew my Aunt Beverly was 50 years old or a little older Aunt Teresa was my mother's baby sister and would have been 55 years old if she was still living. Aunt Teresa, whom my sister was named after, passed away July 8, 2008. **RIP Auntie I Love You Always and Forever**

One day I seen pictures on my timeline on Facebook my Aunt Sylvia liked and shared the picture, the caption read, "Look at my baby sister. I love her so much." I looked at the picture, and right away I saw my mother and Aunt Teresa in Aunt Beverly. Tears streamed down my face I liked the pictures, sent her a friend request and inboxed her through messenger.

It was January 13, 2016 my inbox read "OMG YOUR MY AUNTIE!!!!!!!!!!!!!!!!!! I'M ZADIE's SON. It's me your nephew Auntie…I deleted a couple of people to make sure you have a spot love … MUAH. Here's my number Auntie 404-***-**** Sam /Lil Robert." I returned back to her page and just stared at all her pictures. It felt good to find my auntie, according to the pictures I had a cousin and she had a little baby. I was ecstatic I couldn't wait until my auntie called me or reached back out!

Months went by while school was in session and I forgot about my auntie. In April my cousin Brittany, my Aunt Beverly's daughter, reached out. She was Facebook friends with my Aunt Sylvia and cousin/brother Troy. We became friends on Facebook and chatted through messenger, she was excited she had another cousin and told me a little about her and I told her a little about me she was in Arkansas too.

Right after that my Aunt Beverly reached out to me she finally replied to my inbox. "Hey. Yes, I'm here," I replied. "Where are you so I can finally meet my auntie!"

Aunt Beverly replied, "Getting ready for one of my good friend's wedding. She will be getting married downtown at the Ferris wheel tonight at 8:45 p.m. I can't wait to see you nephew." Then she called!

When my phone rang and I saw the 404 area code I knew it was her because I had almost every number that called my phone stored. I answered "Hello?" she said "Hey nephew this yo Auntie." She even sounds like my Aunt Teresa. We both laughed. Aunt Beverly said, "Hey look, I'm getting ready now so we can head downtown. Meet me down there by the Ferris wheel."

I said, "I sure will, love." And just like that we hung up. The conversation was short but amazing.

I was finally about to meet my Aunt for the first time in my life it was May 7, 2016. The Auburn Fest was going on downtown at Centennial Olympic Park, Clinton went along with me I was nervous but I wasn't nervous. I felt relieved my Aunt had been on my Facebook page she liked certain pictures that let me know she knew about my life. She liked pictures of Clinton and I, she liked pictures of my books and pictures of my molesters I had posted. I knew my aunt was going to be accepting and down to earth.

Clinton and I arrived downtown around 10 p.m. it was kind of breezy from the water fountains at Centennial Olympic Park. We walked around the park and bought some Starburst from one of the vendors. Soon as I took a selfie of us my aunt called and they were walking towards the Ferris wheel I didn't even have a chance to hang up before we both spotted each other at the same time.

We both were smiling super hard and almost ran toward one another we hugged each other tight. Looking at her and hugging her in person I felt I just hugged my mother, Aunts Sylvia, Denise, Teresa and even Aunt Sheri they all looked a like they were sisters indeed. Aunt Beverly said, "Look at my nephew, ya'll this is my nephew, my sister's son!" The ladies she was with hugged and greeted me I introduced her to Clinton and said, "Aunt Beverly this is my boyfriend Clinton" my auntie said, "Baby I know who he is" I said, "YYYYEEESSSSS" and we laughed again.

She told me she came to Atlanta for her best friend's wedding that was like her niece they all looked pretty in their orange sleeveless dresses and stilettos my auntie was killing the game. Clinton took a couple of pictures of us I posted them right away to Facebook and tagged my aunt and cousins in them.

Aunt Beverly asked did we want to join the party at the Ferris wheel grounds and sit at the tables along with them. I told her no everyone was dressed up and Clinton and I had on jeans and gym shoes. I wanted her to enjoy herself that was the reason she came here to Atlanta I was just ecstatic to finally meet her. She made me promise to come to the reception afterwards and I did. I walked away with the best feeling in the world that night. I had just met my auntie for the first time in my life at the age of 37 years old.

CHAPTER 5

MY JUDY ON DUTY

Heavenly Father, I thank you so much for bringing Miyasha into my life. Miyasha and I go back to Dallas Texas from August to December 2010. The most important thing I will be forever grateful for is Miyasha being there for me while I lived in Dallas. That part of my life was crazy and it's even crazier how life turned out.

I met Miyasha through Damion, Damion and Price had become friends when I left Dallas, Texas. Miyasha is Damion's cousin she was also friends with Price. When Miyasha and I first met she called me her hubby, she said I looked like a dude she used to fuck. I learned right away Miyasha was a very blunt person.

Miyasha, Damion and I use to ride around in North Dallas listening to different songs and singing some of the same songs over and over again. Brandy's album "Human" got me through a lot while living in Dallas I was heart broke, I was lost. Brandy's music got me through many, many nights. I think one night riding around the town we listened to every track on the album and knew the words; we sang our poor hearts out.

I believe Miyasha and Damion felt the pain I was going through the pain was hard to shake I think the pain was worse and lasted longer because I didn't want to let Price go. Just about every night I found myself riding from where I lived to their side of the town in North Dallas. They were all the friends I had there other than Tion, Brennan and my roommate/ little brother BJ. They were all I knew other than Price and the men he was fucking.

If we weren't riding around going different places and seeing Dallas we were sitting over Miyasha's house eating, play cards, and sitting outside in the front of the house. I also can't forget we did a lot of "boy watching" there were a lot of men who lived in Miyasha's apartment complex and they were always trying to get at her and always by her place.

If Miyasha wasn't cooking Damion was in the kitchen cooking, they were truly southern with southern hospitality. They would cook neck bones, pig feet, collard greens, hog maws and everything else from the south. I wasn't used to eating they always made sure I was full though I was hardly eating I wasn't in my right mind.

I use to use Miyasha to get numbers from guys. I would tell them she was my sister and wanted to talk to them. They would give her their number, but I never called I did it because I wanted to know if I still had it, could I pull a straight dude like I used too. They knew what was up!

I will never forget going to Inspiring Body of Christ (IBOC) church where I found my strength. I didn't feel a strong presence from GOD before but I felt him every time I entered IBOC. GOD never left me! I'd stray away Miyasha and Damion would always lead me back to him. After we would leave church we always went to "South Dallas Café" to eat, it became our Sunday ritual.

I was going to write my story in a book. Wilhelmina said Atlanta is the place and suggested that I move to Atlanta. I remember when I was preparing to leave Dallas and move to Atlanta, Damion and Miyasha set up a surprise birthday and going away party for me at "Dave & Busters" on my birthday.

Everyone was there I met throughout the four months of living in Dallas from Miyasha, Damion, Tion, Brennan and Miyasha's children. We all ate, played games and sat and talked. I loved the atmosphere and I loved my friends for being there. I felt so alone at that time although I was surrounded by love and my pain wasn't as unbearable. I was out of the hospital now for a month after being beaten, robbed and nearly car jacked, yet GOD was good and I couldn't even complain.

* * * * *

Miyasha has 2 little boys and was a single parent. This chick was on her grind with 2 jobs and a rapper might I add an excellent rapper, the chile can really Rap and I loved it. Miyasha has a testimony. When I say she showed me how life can be rough and you can turn it around, she did just that.

Through her struggles I found inspiration, she is my motivation, Miyasha's story went like this and that's why I call her "My Judy on Duty!" Miyasha moved to Atlanta from Dallas in 2015 definitely starting from the bottom she didn't allow her situation to break her and instead she was empowered by it.

MIAYSHA'S STORY IN HER OWN WORDS...

I've always wanted to do music ever since I was in middle school writing songs singing and rapping with my best friend talking about shit like we were grown-ups. My first time in the studio was off the chain and everybody was giving me my props. It eventually got to the point where the niggas even hated on me and would wait to hear my verse before they even started writing so I would not out do them at that point I knew I had a real talent for it. I went through a completely different type of journey trying to provide another type of lifestyle for children and went through all type of struggles.

I ended being put on child support when I asked my baby daddy to get my son temporarily because I was trying to move I was not comfortable with him being where I was living at the time. When he decided to put me on child support I was in my new spot working two jobs and we rotated my son each week between the two of us I know he only did it out of spite. I cried like a baby and was shocked that the judge would actually take his side and he tried to change his mind in court but at that point it was up to the state. Poor me huh? Hell nah!

I had to keep it pushing because I knew he would need me soon as things got bad with the chick he was with that was trying to play mommy to MY son! She did not really love my son she was just trying to snag him but soon as she felt like he was not catering to her the way she felt he should she did not give a damn about my son. Things changed and my son ended up back with me but I was still paying child support and could not get off unless I went to court for a custody battle. I did not know what else to do because I needed my son to be with me. For a while I pretty much paid double to take care of him.

My baby daddy decided to give me the child support card but would do vindictive shit like cancel the card and have a new one sent to him whenever he got upset. He pretty much had a chain around my neck that he could pull whenever he felt like it. I had so much hate in my heart for him. He took me through a lot of drama. He told the child support office that my child lived with him but just goes to school near me.

I moved on the other side of town about an hour and a half away he called the police and tried to take my baby away saying that I kidnapped him. The police did not fall for that because he did not have any paper work that showed he had custody. There was nothing they could do anyway they do not get involved in civil matters and would have only notified the court that I was not in compliance with the paperwork if in fact there was such in place. I thought in my mind sorry about your luck boo, you tried it!

Those type of situations went on for a while I continued to struggle because I still had my other son I was taking care of too and child care was not cheap. I was going through struggle after struggle and was still in church paying my tithes trying to do everything right and getting absolutely nowhere. I had faith in GOD that he was going to create change in my life for me and my children I got involved with this prayer line and begin calling in every morning.

A few months later I did not have anywhere to live and my children were gone for the winter break. I did not make enough money at my job to really afford an apartment anyway with all of the expenses I had I had a decision to make. It was the first week of January in 2013 I went to an extended stay and paid for two weeks and then gave myself a week to find a better job I know it sounds crazy but I had no other option but to go for it.

The weekend before I went to look for a job I had to go pick up my boys from my mom's house. About 45 minutes into our drive back home my alternator went out. It was freezing cold outside and my phone was only charged enough for me to call my mom and let her know what happened but she did not know my exact location only the area. I kept trying to stop people to use their phone but I could not get anyone's attention. Finally a guy drove by he helped and let me use his phone which was right on time because my mom, aunt, and cousin were right down the street headed in the opposite direction.

We left my car there and came back the next day I had to pay for a used alternator and pay to get it fixed all when I decided to quit my job. It was late before I got it fixed. I left that Tuesday morning already a day behind on my job hunt. I went hard while the boys were at school. By Thursday I was thinking, "Okay GOD, I don't have much time now." I picked the boys up from school and got a job from a staffing agency that saw my resume online. I went in for an interview with them for a client that was looking for workers.

The accounting manager got them on the phone for me took me into his office let me sit in his chair and let me talk to them. I asked them what they were looking for and then I told the lady on the other end that I've done everything there looking for and it equates to what they needed. She scheduled an interview with me right then and there before even seeing my resume! I interviewed an hour later with three people and was hired on the spot paying $4.00 more than my old job!

After my time was up at the extended stay I begged my step mother to live there until I found a spot she was hesitant but she helped me and I was grateful. I was still a part of the prayer line which conflicted with my music because I kept being told I was an evangelist and would minister etc.

I gave up music out of ignorance because I thought that was what GOD wanted me to do I thought he wanted me to do music in Atlanta. I moved in my new apartment in Arlington Texas but only for six months because I was planning to move again. I understand it probably doesn't make much since I was now stable. I was trying to move but I had to do what I thought was right to live my life's purpose.

The months went by and I left headed for Atlanta under the impression that I had a place and a job I cried many tears of joy ready to start my new journey. The house was not ready yet and I was in the owners other house with her waiting to move in when the house was available. I had been there for about three weeks and my children were enrolled in a charter school. A very long story short I was not going to be able to move into the house and my job fell through too.

I was sick to my stomach I remember this particular night like no other night. It was like GOD was calling my name to talk to me like he would always do when he needed my attention. The lights were off and the doors were closed I was on my knees crying out to GOD thinking that it was all over. I knew me and my children would be homeless again right when I thought all I had been through already was over.

God kept speaking to me saying this is not the end this is the beginning and this is your new beginning Miyasha. I cried and cried and cried that night but I knew what I had to do. I had already packed up everything in the car and my children were sleeping. All I could think about was how they were in a bed sleeping comfortably and stable and how the next day all of that was going to change that shit hurt so freaking bad. I felt so empty like where do I go from here after I had went through so much already. My children were in a great school, catching the bus in the morning, making friends, like all of this was about to be over and that was all I could think about.

The next day about 4:30 a.m., I headed out to Atlanta to find a shelter all of them were full and I could not get any help. I finally found one that had openings and it was the worse place ever. I went to the office and sat there for about 4 hours before getting in the **System** the office was full. Afterwards I took the boys to a restau-

Why Did We Meet? — It Wasn't' By Choice

rant to eat so it wouldn't look like we were going through. When we got back we had to stand in line and get on the shower list and wait in the hall until our names were called. I did not know the office would also be the same place we slept. When they pulled out those little bitty ass plastic mats I went and got a spot. This big bitch came in there and said rudely "Ma'am I got five kids!"

I said "Okay what does that mean?" She said "They were we sleep!" I was about to get real fly until I realized she had found a spot for us elsewhere because she already had her stuff over there. We did not get cover or anything and I was scared to go to sleep I literally saw bed bugs crawling and was about to lose my mind. The next morning we got up and put all the office chairs back up before breakfast at the food kitchen. There were homeless people all down the street, prostitutes, crack heads etc. The boys and I were walking down the sidewalk nervous as hell going to the orientation by the food kitchen.

I met some people that were helpful and tried to tell me about how to get in a better shelter etc. The next morning there were people out there handing out water and snacks I did not know they were from the mayor's office. Mark Henderson gave me his cell and Cassandra Edmond was my case worker. Mark asked me if I could be at the office around 10:30 a.m. and I said yes. I went to the Major's office by bus because I was nervous to drive I had not paid my insurance. I got there and Cassandra asked me about my experience and everything that happened. She told me that I was not going back and that she was sending me to another shelter.

I left and got back to realize that my car was gone with everything in it we were left with nothing but the clothes on our back thankfully I had all of our paperwork and identification on me. Mark dropped me off at the Shelter that evening we had our own beds and a good meal. The next day this other girl and her kids came and she was *cool. She took me to church with her the next day and her pastor ministered to me. He told me that I would not be at this place for long and that God was feeding me in a new way. He also said that it was my season of wealth and kept reassuring me that I wouldn't be at this place for long.*

So many times I cried being there. I would walk to the library with my boys until I got them enrolled in the school up the street. I thought on what the pastor said about it being my season of wealth. This was my life and I did not have time to play hell I was going through real shit. One day at the park I sat at the table and was just thinking. I was listening to this song on my phone and thought about my music and realized that I was in Atlanta Georgia and could definitely go after what I wanted and let the religious people think what they want about me.

I was at the shelter almost three weeks until my supposed to be mentor at the time decided to extend his home to me and my children. I was a little uncomfortable because I knew his wife was insecure and had certain thoughts toward me. It did not matter how much she smiled at me and tried to talk to me I knew something was not right. Things were so hectic there; I felt that I was under a microscope. They would say things to me like "my thoughts were very loud and they felt my energy."

They would also say that people called them about me saying "I had unresolved issues in my family and needed to go back home and fix them and that was why I was stagnant." I recognized the manipulation! First you tell me GOG has given you the grace to allow me to stay there and then you say GOD says you have to go home like make up your mind already. When they realized I peeped game they told me that "I am so prophetic in nature they want me to have a balance and not take things the wrong way." No, they just want me to believe everything they say.

They convinced me to let my boys go back with my mom just until I get some things situated which I actually thought was a good idea. After I agreed they put me out and said that it was because they were only letting me live there because of the kids. Ha! Ain't that some shit?! Me and the boys traveled on the mega bus to meet my mom. On my way back I thought about all I would do to make sure I get on.

I was in Memphis waiting on my bus to Atlanta and met some cool people that were waiting on a bus to Dallas. I was telling them how I had just moved from there and was telling them about me getting ready to pursue music etc. Of course they wanted to hear something so I let them hear a song I had done. It was a lot of people out there waiting with me in the little tiny stop as well as people outside that did not have any room to sit.

I played the song and everybody got quiet. When the song was done everybody kept saying how they were not expecting me to be good and how I sound like I'm already on. They were asking for my number trying to keep it contact with me like I was a super star! That was my first sign from GOD that it was for me. That was my lane, and where I would lay my foundation in Atlanta no more doubts, fears, and caring what others thought.

I got back to Atlanta and moved in with Sam. He gave me a place of peace, a place where I could really relax and let my hair down I love him so much for that. It was only then when I was able to begin enjoying my experience in Atlanta. I got a job, another car, and eventually got my own place. As of today I am proud to say that I still have a great job with benefits, my own place and getting other things started.

I am almost finished with my EP that I'm getting ready to drop and they are fucking with ya' girl out here on this music I know I am about to kill the scene! I went through a lot and I don't doubt that I may still go through but baby when you have already hit the bottom you can't go anywhere but up! Stay tuned though, my story is still being written. To be continued...

* * * * *

    Timothy, Dominique and I went to New Jersey for TaQuan's birthday party in January 2015. I met TaQuan through Timothy he is part of the circle we all have. It was TaQuan's 32nd birthday and he was having an extravagant party celebrating so much. TaQuan and his fiancé David moved from Atlanta back home to New Jersey where they both received promotions within their field of work. TaQuan working for the mayor of Newark and David got a higher position within the United States Postal Service.

    School was out for the winter break I drove the four hours to South Carolina where Timothy lived we took my car for the trip. Dominique was already at Timothy's house when I arrived she was a coworker and friend of Timothy. We all split the gas for the road trip there and back. Timothy and I agreed a while ago we would take each other's cars on the trips, Timothy had to do 2 trips when he purchased his next car I used my car twice already.

    There was no snow from Atlanta to South Carolina but it was freezing. I felt like I was back in Minnesota during the winter months every time we stopped for gas or for bathroom breaks. Timothy and I sang our hearts out as we generally do on every road trip and every time we're together Dominique slept the majority of the ride. No later than we crossed the state line from Virginia into Washington, DC, it started snowing.

A couple of months before I was speaking with Adonis and #26 I told both of them I was coming to New Jersey to visit friends both of them made me promise I would visit when I was driving through their state of Maryland. Around 4 a.m. we reached Baltimore I'd been speaking with Adonis ever since we hit Virginia. When crossed into Baltimore Adonis gave me the address where to meet him he was just getting off work.

I was so excited to see Adonis, I loved this man since the first day I saw him I knew he loved me. He's married now to someone and still wanted me. He never stopped doing what he was doing for me when we started back talking he was sending money and naked pictures every chance he got. Technically he was straight but his new wife wanted to see him get fucked by a man and I was the man he wanted it to happen with.

Adonis gave me the address to Wal-Mart it was right around the corner from his job. I was ecstatic I was about to see Adonis for the first time since 2005. He talked me through the direction where he was parked in the parking lot. As soon as I parked he stepped out of his truck before I could put my car in park. I got out of the car and Adonis hugged me so hard he picked me up off the ground. He couldn't stop saying how much he missed and loved me and I was saying the same in return.

Timothy and Dominique were just looking with their mouths wide open neither of them could believe how fine he was let alone how straight he looked they were not ready for any of that. I explained to them our love before we saw him I wanted them to see it for themselves too. Adonis and I went into Wal-Mart he grabbed a couple of items and Timothy and Dominique waited in the car.

We were walking through Wal-Mart and pushing each other like school kids.

Timothy called my phone and said they were hungry and I was too. Adonis told me to tell them once we left there to just follow him to a Diner. When we left out of Wal-Mart I got in the truck with Adonis, Timothy and Dominique followed behind us. The entire ride to the Diner neither of us could stop laughing and touching each other. In the Diner Adonis and I sat together and I told Timothy to sit with Dominique at a separate table I wanted as much alone time as possible with him.

Adonis ordered breakfast and I ordered fries and a coke I just gazed at him and talked about old times. Adonis told me he loved me over a thousand times. I started recording him and he began taking pictures of me he still had the same smile and soft touch it was cold outside but I was warm next to him.

As our time was coming to an end it was time for us to get back on the road. Adonis paid for us and we all left the Diner. Adonis walked with us to my car hugged me tight, said I love you and call me when you make it to Jersey then closed the door.

We finally arrived in New Jersey during the worst time possible, it was during 8 a.m. rush hour traffic and it was sleeting and snowing the temperature was 20 degrees but felt like −20. We made it to Dominique's people's house and dropped her off before heading to TaQuan and David's condo in Newark. We stopped down the street from their house at Burger King to get something to eat and take a couple of pictures to post on Facebook letting everyone know we touchdown in Jersey.

We left Burger King initially going to TaQuan's but we were so tired we headed to our hotel for some sleep instead after all we'd been up for over 24 hours. We checked in our hotel at the Comfort

Inn and Suites, the room was beautiful, we always had beautiful hotel rooms whenever we went out of town. TaQuan called us later he and David were also having a gathering at their home.

We woke up after 5 p.m., got dressed and made it to TaQuan's around 7 p.m. TaQuan and David had a house full of friends, we all ate, played spades and got drunk. Afterwards Timothy and I went back to the hotel I had the munchies something fierce so we decided to get something to eat. We drove around the city and found nothing it was almost 5 a.m. everything was closed. We ended up right next door to the hotel at a gas station. I brought 2 polishes and a bag of chips back in the hotel room; I demolished my food and crashed.

At 7 a.m., Timothy woke me up for the complimentary breakfast in the hotel. You would have thought they would only have Danishes, donuts and juice but this hotel had pancakes and waffles you make yourself, bacon, sausage, ham, eggs, oatmeal, Danishes and donuts and even cereal. It also came with apple juice, orange juice and bottles of water. I love this hotel!

We went back to sleep after we ate and didn't wake up until the afternoon. We got dressed and hit the streets, it was close to 9 p.m. and we knew we had to head back to the hotel and get ready for the party. We shopped a little before Kevin called.

Kevin is also a friend in our circle, he and I got into it almost a year ago over his nephew. I wrote about the full story in "How It All Happened" but we talked through our issues and made up. Kevin and his boyfriend Quinton were there for me through every surgery and during the time I had attempted suicide. Usually I would be done with someone depending on the reason for the fall out, Kevin is like family I couldn't throw our friendship away.

I told Kevin we were about to pick up some Mexican food then we would pick him up from the train station. Timothy told Kevin to catch the train and get off on the exit near our hotel. I asked Kevin if he wanted to eat before hanging up, we picked up our food then Kevin from the train station and headed back to the room.

Kevin flew to New York from Atlanta because he didn't want to do the 16 hour drive. We got back to the hotel ate, showered and then changed clothes the party was at the "Taste Venue" downtown Newark. By the time we all were ready it was a little after 10 p.m., the party started at 9 p.m. just like black people running on CP time (colored people) we were running a little late. **Side Stare**

We parked in a lot down from the building, the parking attendant asked if we were attendees of the party, we told him yes he gave us a "Special tag" and directed us to the building. OMG talking about feeling like you have celebrity status! There were so many heavy hitters from Jersey there, TaQuan knew people in big places.

Flat screen TV's hung from the walls and TaQuan had pictures of all his family and friends displayed on the screens throughout the room. I was in four pictures making me feel special! My outfit was cute, I had on a blue fitted button up shirt, dark blue jeans, and a Nike fitted blue and black NYC cap with black Nike boots.

TaQuan had a DJ, food, lots of miniature alcohol bottles with "chess pieces on top" as party favors, and a cash bar. We didn't have time to sit down with TaQuan introducing us to everyone, dancing and drinking we stayed on our feet. We all danced together "The Circle" Timothy, Kevin, David, TaQuan and I, it felt good to have a strong circle of friends who are all heading to the top, all I could remember next was walking to the car around 3am, where did the time go?

The next morning at 6 a.m. Timothy and I woke up, showered and ate the free breakfast before getting our share of free hotel towels and calling for extras before we hit the road. We called David and TaQuan while on the highway and said our good-byes and until next time. We picked up Dominique and we were off.

I called #26 to let him know we were going to be in Baltimore in about 3 hours and to text me the address where he was. I was keeping my promise of making sure to visit him. #26 lived in NYC but was visiting with family in Baltimore. I called him when we arrived at the hotel he was staying at -------- I'll pick up later about what happened.

* * * * *

Miyasha and I lived together at this point she'd seen me somewhat date both Anthony and Antonio. I was playing the field dating both of them at the same time while I was messing around with other people too. I was playing the field until I found a match, I wasn't going to settle with someone who couldn't give me at least half of what I offered and wanted. Let me stop lying, if you couldn't give me everything I wanted and I wanted ALL the 3 Cs —Crib, Car and Career.

Anthony was the first person Miyasha had seen me with after dating Price. I honestly was kind of nervous introducing her to him. I met Anthony at Wal-Mart, he was this tall midnight brother with an athletic toned body, braids and a beard, and he caught my attention. It was freezing outside to me and he had on a t-shirt. No it wasn't freezing but it wasn't warm enough for a damn t-shirt plus he smelled like good weed.

I'd smelled like weed too after all I just smoked. I was interested so I asked him where the green at. He looked at me laughed and said, "Shit you tell me where the green at?" We both laughed.

I said, "At the crib"

He said, "Mine, too. I'm Anthony, bro."

I said, "I'm Trey, bro," and we shook hands. I asked what his number was so I could hit his line, he gave it to me and said, call my phone. I was calling his phone and he asked what I was about to do. I told him nothing.

Anthony told me to follow him back to his crib and we could smoke one. In my mind I was saying "work bitch work" I didn't know if he was straight or gay I felt the feeling he was about to be gay for me. We got back to his place, which was right around the corner from me, headed in and he took me to his room. He lived with his sister and her children but had his own room.

We started smoking and listening to the radio sitting on some chairs in his room. He was playing the 360 game system, and started asking questions like where I worked, who I lived with, what I like to do and I was asking the same. He said he worked at the peanut butter company up the road as a packager and just bought his car. He was also looking for his own place and had to move in with his sister after his breakup. I was all ears, break up from who I asked my slick ass!

Anthony said he broke up with his boyfriend of three years in my mind I was screaming "YYYYAAAASSSSSS" but my mouth said "I'm sorry to hear that bro" he said it's cool man he moved on already it's time for me to do the same. Anthony asked if I have a boyfriend and I answered no. After the blunt went out I told Anthony I was about to bounce and I would hit him up later we shook hands and I left.

I thought Anthony was sexy but I honestly didn't want a chocolate boyfriend I really didn't like dark skin men but I was attracted to him and I wanted to try it out. The next day Anthony called and asked if I want to catch a movie. Of course I said yes and he asked my address, I gave it to him and he came over so I could ride with him. When he walked in Miyasha's eyes got big, she said you so cute and chocolate with emphasis on the chocolate part I said ain't he and we all laughed, his smile was beautiful and lite up the room.

We left for the movies and smoked on the way there. In the theater we sat next to each other and he rubbed on my thighs and had me on brick in the theater. I told him if he didn't stop we were going to have to leave and go home, Anthony replied, "Let's go," and just like that he wasted his money and the movie had just started.

Anthony was cute and sexy but he wasn't for me he was a gym shoe head and had to have every pair of Jordans and it irritated my soul. I'm a shoe whore but this was something different, this man had a toothache and didn't have dental insurance and had to pay to have his tooth pulled or a root canal. He went through pain for a whole two weeks because he spent his money on a pair of Jordans and had to wait until payday again to pay for his tooth; it pissed me off and let me know where his priorities were and where he stood with me.

I started messing around with Antonio in November of 2014, he was a tall athletic a red bone, 6'2, bow legged, hairy, dread locks with some pretty ass feet. I met him off the Jack'd app he lived alone, had a car and worked for Comcast but I knew he was a hoe the dick was too good, big and he looked too damn fine not to be.

The first night I hooked up with Antonio was on his birthday November 10th, we exchanged numbers over the app and he called me. He sounded manly and I had the feeling we all get and I was single. I showered and headed out to his place. He stayed 7 minutes, from me per the GPS, I called him when I pulled into his apartment complex and he directed me through.

His door was slightly open and he was standing in the doorway I walked in we shook hands and hugged, he was even hotter in person. We sat on the couch and Antonio offered me some Tequila. We drank, smoked and before long we were kissing. He kissed me sensual and deep he rubbed his warm hands all over my body while kissing me at the same time.

Before I knew it I was naked in this mans bed and he was on top of me. After a couple of hours of foreplay and great sex we passed out. He held me the entire night and we didn't even roll over one time in our sleep. I felt comfortable in his arms. When I woke up the next morning I came to the realization he would be a sex buddy along with Anthony and that's it, that's all. I found myself sleeping with him until I met my boyfriend Clinton in July of 2015.

CHAPTER 6

THE DATING SCENE

Oh boy, dating was something else in Atlanta it seemed like everyone I was interested in was feminine men and those I weren't were masculine. Atlanta was a big circle and everyone knew everyone meaning everyone slept with one another. AIDS/HIV and syphilis is running rampant, just about every dude I came in contact with has AIDS/HIV or had never been tested.

I believe those who stated they never been tested had never been tested because they feared they were indeed positive. Between all the sex parties, feminine men, broke men, men that did not have the 3 C's (Crib, Car, Career) and men who were not attractive, it was going to be hard to have a relationship. In the meantime and in between time I was going to play the field.

Atlanta does have a lot of sexy brothers and they were there for the pickings, the only problem was everyone already picked through them. After 3 failed relationships with Price, #26 and #14 I was done with love. I knew I really wanted to be in love we all want to be loved by someone. I went through a lot of frogs to finally get to my prince and I'm not referring to looks. I was never looking for love I allowed love to find me. Throughout this entire process of elimination there were the occasional hook ups and everyone I hooked up with was HIV POSITIVE — I DO LITERALLY MEAN EVERYONE, EXCEPT #26 & #14!

* * * * *

I met KJ on the chat line Adam4Adam January 2014. I met all the guys on either Adam4Adam or Jack'd these websites are for gay men. They are generally sites for a quick hook up; some people actually meet their mate on some of these apps. There were other apps like grinder and tender but I stuck with what I knew. The apps I were on have majority black men the other websites were a lot of white men I loved my brothers.

KJ was a year older than me and also a Sagittarius. He had his own everything and all of the 3 Cs: a Dodge Charger, a nice home and a good job in management. KJ was a thick football player type guy I honestly didn't like thick guys with a stomach but he was solid at 220 pounds, 6'2", a red bone with a cut low fade. I was trying things I didn't like I usually went for the athletic type.

We always want what we can't have and what's good for us we don't want. KJ was very much into me cool and nice. Our schedules seemed to always conflict I was in school and he was working at night I was either studying or with my friends. I wanted a relationship but I wasn't ready for commitment. I kind of still wanted to have fun KJ wanted commitment and I couldn't give him that. We really didn't have a chance to date and were just sex partners. It was cool while it lasted but I couldn't give him what he wanted and after a while we slowly went our separate ways.

*****

I met Jerrod next on Jack'd. He seemed to give the straight man thuggish vibe on the app he was dark skin and skinny. We chatted one day when I was over my straight homie Onsemious' house in College Park. Jack'd always give people within a 5 mile radius from you. Jerrod wanted to smoke and match a blunt I told him once I got back to the crib I would hit him up. I asked did he have a car and he said no he could take the bus. I knew right then and there if anything went down between us he would just be a hook up and nothing more.

When I got home I texted and he called right away. He was about to head out to get on the train before it stopped running for the night. In my mind I thought if the train stopped running for the night that meant either he's going to spend the night or I was going to take him back home. I asked what he had planned once he got over here Jerrod replied he just wanted to chill. I already knew what that meant and I didn't have Netflix. He really wanted to smoke and have sex I was down with that I was single doing single things.

Once Jerrod made it to the train station on my side of town he called for me to pick him up and instantly I was turned off. I arrived at the train station and he walked toward the car after I told him I was pulling up. Jerrod was cute, a little taller than me around 6 feet tall and about 140 pounds, he was a tall dark skin skinny thug. In person I couldn't tell he was gay I liked that about a man. We came back to my house smoked and watched TV, after our second blunt he pulled out a bottle of Apple Crown from his back pack he was all prepared to "chill."

The sun begun to come up and he began to make his move. He stood up and took all his clothes off and said "isn't this what you want?" I wasn't all attracted to him but he wasn't about to be my man I stood up and stripped, too. I directed him to the bedroom and we went at it. He was a true freak.

The next day when it was time to take him back to the train station he asked could I take him home he didn't have train fare. I asked how much did it cost for the train and he said $2.50. *Wait, what?* I thought. *$2.50?! Yo ass don't have $2.50 but you have weed and alcohol?!* I said no more and gave him $5 and told him to hit me once he made it home.

Soon as he called me and said he made it home, I hung up and blocked his ass from Jack'd and my phone. I didn't want a bum ass dude that didn't have shit to offer me and their priorities all fucked up Price taught me all too well enough!

* * * * *

JR was a cutie and sexy as fuck, the only problem is that he was too damn young at 22. He lied when we first chatted on Jack'd. His profile stated he was 27, 5'8 and 150 pounds. He was actually 5'6" weighing 150 pounds but was cut the fuck up, bow legged, hairy, a red bone with a low cut fade, muscular and the hardest southern accent. JR only talked about wanting a relationship while we chatted. He was short, very short at 5'6". I have never had sex with, let alone even dated, someone that short.

We made plans to go out on a date and meet for the first time at Los Arcos Mexican Restaurant. JR asked me what I liked to eat and when I said Mexican food he said that was his favorite and picked the spot right away for us to meet. I noticed instantly he was super aggressive I wanted to meet the next day he was adamant on meeting later on that day. JR said, "I'll come and pick you up if I have to I see something I like!"

That turned me on I didn't turn him down I started getting ready shaving, ironing and taking a shower. I put together a little outfit nothing too cute it was hot outside it was almost the start of the summer in June 2014. I was getting dressed when JR called and said he was ready to leave out. I told him to text me the address and I would leave out in a few minutes. I made my way out the door and headed to the restaurant it was only 11 minutes away we both stayed by each other according to Jack'd. JR was less than a mile from me.

I pulled up to the restaurant and parked right away. I spotted JR standing at the door of the restaurant he was smiling hard when I pulled into my parking spot. He walked up to my car and opened the door I stepped out and he closed the door behind me we hugged and he said nice to finally meet you dude I said nice to meet you too. I was stuck on the fact that he was really short in person I didn't think he was going to be that short though.

We headed inside the restaurant and he hurried up behind me to open the door. The hostess sat us and gave us our menus we began to have small talk and he gave me a couple of suggestions from the menu. By it being my first time I told him to go ahead and order me something good he asked was I sure and I said yes just don't order me anything with beans. He ordered our food with an order of margaritas.

We had short talk until our food came he was very interesting he worked two jobs, one at Wal-Mart and the other at Footlocker. My eyebrows kind of rose up for a second I wasn't knocking anyone's form of income but I was looking for the blue collar type guy.

He was from Georgia and was an only child. I asked him what type of car he had because I saw him standing at the door verses getting out of his vehicle JR said he drove a Camry.

He went on to state he lived alone I liked that he had all the 3 Cs. After we were done eating JR asked the waitress for the check. When she returned I took out my card so I could pay for my half. I figured since we were just meeting we were going Dutch. JR said, "What are you doing?"

I said, "Paying for my food!"

JR said, "A real man pays the check. Put your card up!" He didn't have to tell me twice, back in my pocket went my card fast as hell. He paid and we headed out the door.

JR walked me back to my car and opened the door as I unlocked it. He was all smiles. He said, "It feels good to have this time with you."

I replied, "Mutual, bro, mutual."

We hugged and he said, "Call me once you make it home."

All the way home I thought about him. Like anyone else when you first meet someone you think of them in your future and how life would be.

JR and I were talking for a couple of weeks before we finally had sex. We hung out at the bowling alley and went to the movies. I even spent the night over his house and he was a perfect gentleman and didn't try to have sex with me he just held me the entire night and kept saying this is what he wanted, I loved being held. His apartment was nice he had all the latest electronics and even a projector screen for his TV set up in the living room.

One day he had gotten off work from Footlocker and called me. He said he didn't have to go to his second job until later at midnight he was working from midnight to 8 a.m. He asked if I had anything to eat, he was hungry and wanted to stop over. I told him to come through. When he walked through the door I instantly got hard. JR had on a wife beater, basketball shorts with no underwear and flip flops with no socks he had the cutest feet.

JR came through the door hugged, caressed and kissed me. He kissed and walked me to my room. He laid me down on the bed and began to take my clothes off. I must have had my eyes closed while we walked to the bedroom because when I opened my eyes while lying on bed JR was naked. He started to lick my body from head to toe. He was actually licking my feet and sucking on my toes. I wanted him bad as ever because he really had me turned on.

All during sex he kept saying, "I love you." I was stuck I couldn't say that back I just moaned the entire time. JR was long winded and he made love to me nice and slow at first. After we were done we laid and cuddled up until we fell asleep. His lying ass didn't come over because he was hungry he came over because he was horny.

A couple of months had passed when JR and I went out to eat at Olive Garden. I ordered us some wine and the waiter asked us for our IDs. The waiter gave us our IDs back and I asked him could I see his. I didn't verify anything he told me far as his name, age and birthdate. He gave me his ID and started laughing. I was looking at it and immediately noticed his birthday was September of 1994. "Bro, you are not no damn 27!"

He laughed and said, "I'm 21 going on 22. In a few days that shouldn't be a problem!"

I told him, "I am 35 years old and I have a nephew that's older than you. You are the same age as my niece!"

JR didn't care and said age was nothing but a number. He said, "Didn't I fuck you like I'm a grown man?"

I was silent because he wasn't lying, but I knew in my heart I couldn't be with anyone that young. I learned my lesson from being with Price. I feel like younger dudes don't really know what they truly want. They want things for the moment and I wanted things for a lifetime. Although everything about JR was on point, I still cut him off. He lied from the start about something simple. I was not doing liars and I left them where they stood!

* * * * *

Mike was a really cute guy we met at the clinic where I spoke. When he gave me his number, the first night we talked until the sun came up, his conversation was excellent he knew what he wanted in life. He was looking for a relationship, school was starting back in September 2014 and I knew my schedule was going to be hectic. I told Mike right away I wanted a relationship too but we would have to take it slow.

Mike was cool with that he worked for a non-profit organization and said his schedule was hectic too. He spoke at different events about AIDS/HIV he is also a part of the Big Brother program to help the youth here in Atlanta. I was attracted to Mike; he was a red bone, my height at 5'9" about 160 pounds with a very deep voice.

We never dated our schedules prevented us from meeting a lot. Some days he would be in meetings, we would text until he got home then we would talk the night away. He would spend nights at my house and leave the next day for work, he worked Tuesday through Sunday he had no time off on the weekends which sucked.

I didn't like spending the night over at his house he had roommates and they would knock on the door constantly. His roommates were other gay men they were very flamboyant and would always flirt with me when I came over, talk about irritating. Mike didn't have a car he was always taking the bus or asking me to take him somewhere or pick him up. He would offer gas but at times I didn't care about the gas money I didn't want to start being his personal Uber.

I guess Mike noticed after a couple of weeks I was hesitant to take him anywhere or pick him up. He called himself trying to call me out he called one night and was upset and was trying to chastise me. Mike told me if you're in a relationship you are supposed to help your mate, I told him I definitely understood but we were not in a relationship we were just fucking.

Mike was very upset with my response he told me I was going to be mad once he walked away and if he did he was through. I told him that was fine with me, he proceeded to tell me he didn't want to date anyone that didn't know how to talk properly anyway or respect their man! I was confused by the statement and asked him what he meant. Mike told me whenever I text him I always called him bro or dude I use the letter U instead of the word you and I was supposed to submit to him!

I told him he was just pissed because I didn't want to talk to him in the way he wanted and I don't submit to anyone! I didn't want to talk to him because he dressed like he was a cowboy 24-fucking-7! Mike would wear his cowboy boots with everything he wore all the way from jeans, slacks to denim shorts. I told him I wanted to date a brother not a cowboy and not to mention I wasn't a taxi and hung up!

* * * * *

Next was Brandon it was mid-October and the men here in Atlanta were something else. All I could do was laugh at them I knew I had some issues but some of those people had issues I didn't want to even try putting up with. I was at school one day and my Jack'd had been going crazy with all the notifications.

My phone always went crazy by the school there were a lot of gay, bisexual confused men in the area of the West end. This guy's picture had body for days from his profile and was a red bone. A red bone dude was my kryptonite I was a damn sucker for a red bone man. His profile said he was 6'2", 170 pounds and was only looking for masculine men. I liked his profile so I read his message and he was basically just looking for a hook up.

He told me his name was Brandon he was 29, from Chicago and straight! I told him I was at school and I was about to leave to head home. He gave me his number and said to call. I waited until I got to the house and hit him up. He told me he just moved here, lived alone and was bored. I asked did he smoke and he said who doesn't we laughed and I told him I wouldn't be free until later on in the evening.

Brandon was cool with that and told me to hit him up later on then. I took a nap and hit him up around 10 p.m. when I woke up. I called him and he was leaving a bar, he texted me his address I and told him I would leave out in the next 30 minutes. I rolled a blunt and rode out to Brandon's place by my school.

Brandon lived in a gated community. I called him when I pulled up. He gave me the gate code and buzzed me through, I was nervous he said he was straight and he looked thuggish. Although there were news reports of gay men getting robbed by meeting people on Jack'd in the metro area of Atlanta I wasn't nervous from that, I was nervous because of his picture he looked too straight!

I parked and called him back so he could meet me outside. Brandon came down the stairs and met me at the walkway. He shook my hand and told me to follow him. This dude was every bit of straight in my eyes. We went into the apartment which was clean and looked nothing like a gay man's place. He had sports memorabilia hanging from walls, all kinds of Jerseys and even boxed basketballs and baseballs. He took me into a bedroom where he had a movie playing.

We sparked up our blunts and started talking. We talked about where we came from how long we had both been living in Atlanta, the people we came across and his ex-girlfriend. He said his ex-girlfriend found out he was fucking dudes and he didn't want to deal with that so he moved to Atlanta. I asked him his HIV status and he said he was HIV positive but didn't like talking about it. I was lost, but moved on from the conversation. We both were grown and knew what we were about to do as long as he knew I was positive, I was cool.

While we were smoking Brandon started rubbing on me and told me to make myself comfortable and take some clothes off. It was kind of chilly out I had on a jacket, jeans and gym shoes. I told him to do the same I felt like he was taking his clothes off in slow motion so I could see his body he was cut up with a ripped 8-pack.

After we were both naked Brandon started kissing and licking my nipples he sure knew the way to get me in the mood, before long Brandon was inside of me. About a good 20 minutes in it seemed to get even better before I heard the alarm go off. I heard a code being entered into the alarm panel Brandon set by the door. Brandon jumped out of me and ran to the bedroom door and just stood there holding his dick with the condom still on it.

My heart was racing, my mind said, "Bitch put yo got damn clothes on and get the fuck out of here quick fast and in a hurry!" I started putting my clothes on fast as I could I heard footsteps coming towards the bedroom.

I heard a man's voice say, "You are motherfucking kidding me!" Before this man got to the room I had my got damn clothes and shoes already on!

I looked up and there was a dark-skinned, skinny, feminine man standing in the doorway. He was pissed from the look on his face! All I could say was, "Yo, this nicca told me he was straight and single. I had no clue about you, man!"

The man said, "It's cool, just please get the fuck out!" He didn't have to say nothing else. I walked out of there like I was in the marathon about to go for the gold medal!

I got in my car drove right off, looking in the rear view mirror and making sure neither one of their asses was following me. When I got a couple blocks away, I pulled over at the gas station. My shirt was on backwards and I left my underwear, socks, and jacket. My shoes were on the wrong feet. That was a real fucked up situation. I was just glad Brandon's boyfriend didn't walk in on us having sex. I was real glad they had an alarm system. Who knows what may have transpired if not.

I was not with the cheating type of guys and I know how I felt when Price was cheating I just never caught Price in the act. I floated back between JR and KJ. I chilled with either of them whenever I had the urge, they were both nearby they really like me and with them sex was great. I never played with either of their mind, they knew about each other and they also knew about Anthony and Antonio, they were cool with it and so was I. ***Anthony and Antonio didn't know about them or each other.***

Why Did We Meet? — It Wasn't' By Choice

I chilled with KJ and JR until I met Eric in January. I found myself back on the apps after deleting them in October. Between KJ and JR I didn't know who was pushing more for a relationship. I didn't want to get involved with either of them I was basically cheating having sex with them I wasn't going to be able to trust them because of that.

Eric was definitely not my type I was just looking for a loyal consistent cut buddy (Sex partner with no strings attached). Eric was built exactly like KJ weighing 220 pounds solid, bald head and dark skin. He was sexy because he looked straight, he invited me over to his home to have drinks and when I pulled up I was taken back.

Eric has a three-level townhome he had it decked out with the latest furniture wall to ceiling mirrors Italian rugs and flat screen TVs on the walls in every room of the house. There was a Mercedes Benz sitting in the driveway with a new tag on it, this man definitely had every C possible!

We sat in his living room and drank our drinks and talked in front of the lite fireplace, it was cold outside with a balmy temperature of 30 degrees, but it was warm inside his place. Throughout the conversation he kept saying he knew me from somewhere I told him we all have a twin. He said you know it's getting late you might as well spend the night I'm off work tomorrow and if you don't have to work that would be cool.

I didn't work I was good in the hood we took our drinks to the bedroom upstairs and slid in the bed I felt like I had to climb in. We had sex and passed out, Eric's sex was different he was a multiple-cummer I think Eric came about eight to 10 times without stopping. When I woke up Eric wasn't in the bed, the TV was on and the curtains were open. I smelled the aroma of food in the air. Eric was coming up the stairs with plates of food he cooked pancakes, bacon, sausage and eggs.

Damn I was impressed Eric said good morning sleepy head and passed me my plate. We both ate our food and I told him I had to leave shortly after. I left and Eric called me on the phone when I was about 10 minutes away he said, "Hey, you left your hat. You have to come back some time to get it."

I said, "Cool. No problem. I will, bro," and we hung up.

Our relationship was based on good sex; we never hung out other than at his house. One day Eric invited me over and his best friend was there, I'd walked in and thought I seen a ghost. There stood his best friend Trez Atlanta was so damn small I had hooked up with Trez the year before.

Eric introduced us and he immediately saw the tension and asked, "Ya'll know each other?" We both said yes right away, talk about an awkward moment — it was total silence at first. Eric broke the silence by saying, "So, who was better my best friend or me?" Then said, "Wait a minute. This is Trey from the video!"

I said, "Video? What video?"

Eric said, "Trez and I used to be roommates and we had a security system with cameras throughout the house. I saw ya'll having sex. That's where I know you from!"

I was pissed, I was caught on camera and I hadn't even seen it or had a copy. I asked, "Did I do well on camera?"

Eric said, "Hell yes!" We all laughed.

Next thing I knew, we were all in Eric's bed together. The fantasy of wanting two best friends was coming true and I was in the middle, enjoying it all. After it was over I was shocked and surprised. Eric said this was a regular thing for them. That kind of had me jealous. I hated sharing but I knew he wasn't my man.

When I was about to graduate, I realized I really didn't want Eric anymore. I felt I was ready for a relationship. I wanted to be with someone who didn't want to be with anyone else. I wanted to be with someone who had a problem with me being with anyone else. After the night of my graduation and book release party I let Eric go.

I had this party all planned out and Eric was my date, I introduced him to all my family and friends as a friend that's all Eric was to me, he was just a good friend with benefits no one had to know that part except for my closest friends. That night was the last I heard from Eric he never knew where I lived and I blocked his number. I was good for just cutting dudes off with no questions it was like giving them a taste of their own medicine.

CHAPTER 7

DL MEN

Some people thought because they sent me death threats I would stop talking and writing. Well little did they know they were the fuel to my fire I was not going to be intimidated or stopped. I released all of my molester's names, with that came their friends exposing themselves and I didn't even have to say a damn word I simply threw hints! We all know dogs only bark when they are hit. Still to this very day NO LAWSUITS HAVE BEEN FILED! HA!

When bad things happen to people and they don't seek help they end up on drugs, alcohol, having promiscuous sex, catching STDs, AIDS/HIV, stealing, committing crimes, going to jail, attempting or committing suicide and even sometimes dead. These things simply happen because they never spoke about what happened to them and never sought any help.

We have to start paying attention to our children even if they're not yours you still need to pay attention, remember everyone lives in this world together! Nothing ever goes away until it teaches us what we need to know. What we need to know is by us keeping silent these vicious acts against innocent children only continues and worsens with time.

My goal is to share my message all over the world! I want to ensure I speak my truth so our youth never has to speak theirs. If so, I want to be able to help them overcome their problems by giving them coping skills. I want to be booked to speak whenever possible I'm trying to make a difference by making sure my message is heard and changing the law!

No one who's been abused should ever see their abusers walk this earth like nothing has ever happened! I want those naysayers, the naive, and those who are simply in denial to see me going from overlooked to being over booked! I will make a difference. Enough is Enough! If I were lying I would have been sued by now. It's been 5 years and STILL NO LAWSUITS but many death threats!

I'm placing my life on the line to educate people. Unfortunately some of the actual characters I refer to are related to others, are husbands, baby fathers or friends however I didn't pick the roles they play in the books *Eyes Without A Face, How It All Happened*, and my newest release, *Why Did We Meet?*

We have to protect our youth! Some parents are naive, blind and downright dirty. Some parents don't do any research on the men they date and allow them in their homes. Let's be honest for a second, we have too many hoes out here willing to give it up but these monsters seek out our innocent youth!

We see it all the time on the news — Child beat by mom's boyfriend, child pregnant by mom's boyfriend, child molested by mom's boyfriend, child found with semen in them from mom's boyfriend, child found dead from mom's boyfriend." I'm telling you about mom's boyfriend right now. Talk to your kids and ask them questions! Let's all pray that mom's boyfriend hasn't touched your child. How many more victims do we need to WAKE UP?!

I hate I have created enemies for speaking about what happened to me as a child. However I will not be intimidated because people can't deal with the scandalous horrific things they've done to one of GOD's children!

The very first thing I need to do was let people know who my second cousins are that molested me. Sometimes people have to know someone who has a strong connection to you to even fathom some news like being molested. I believe every family has a little incest going on within it. The incest within my family was my cousins and my situation.

My second cousins are my grandfather's nephews from his brothers. My cousin Markell "Kelly" Edmond started off grooming me by giving me candy; wrestling and spending time with me when my mother and brother would leave me home alone. The debacle with my mother's ex-boyfriend Robert "Bob" Jackson had just ended. I was only 10 going on 11 years old when Kelly started molesting me. He lived next door to us with his sister, her son and his older brother.

The very first time he had sex with me he came over and we sat in the living room watching TV. He told me to go in the bedroom so we could wrestle. I was used to wrestling because we did this all the time but this time was very different. This time he placed me in positions that made his dick touch my ass. His dick was hard and he kept rubbing it between the crack of my ass. He told me that his dick was hurt from rubbing against his jeans and pulled down my pants then pulled down his.

Kelly told me to bend over the bed so he could put me in this new position. He placed a pillow in front of me and told me to put my face in it and if it hurt to bite down on the pillow and not scream. He then put some Vaseline on his dick and rubbed his dick against my buttocks. Kelly then gently pushed himself inside of me.

Unlike my other cousin Punkin, I screamed when he first put his dick inside of me, I remember like it was yesterday Punkin telling me, "Shut up and bite the pillow!" I did not like it at all! I didn't even know Punkin. I don't even know my second cousin's Punkin's real name. I don't know anything about him, except he is my grandfather's nephew, he lives in Memphis last I knew and my mother is in contact with him.

I figured Punkin knew about cousin Kelly and that's why he did it to me. After Kelly cam inside me he told me to go in the bathroom and wash up. He walked out the door and I cleaned all the blood up that was between my legs. When my other country second cousin Punkin had sex with me there was blood too. The next morning I woke up and my underwear was full of blood in the back. My mother never questioned the blood and she was the one who did laundry. I always think to myself and ponder on why she never asked about my bloody underwear, I didn't throw them away.

I was already dealing with a lot as a 10 years old child. My mother's boyfriend had molested me, my mother beat me because of it and didn't stop after it, my brother was beating me and now some of my family including my mother and brother were calling me fag/punk/sissy and now my second cousin Kelly was molesting me and my country second cousin Punkin had molested me as well.

It took a long time to forgive both Kelly and Punkin. It hurt me so much because they are my cousins and they knew what was going on within my household. Kelly molested me for a little over two years before Maurice "Munk" Moody took his place by doing the same thing when I was just 12 years old. To this day, I still have a hard time dealing and speaking about my cousins Kelly and Punkin. It took a lot out of me just speaking about it this much.

* * * * *

When people know your heart they support you. I'm not doing any of this to be messy, petty, and vindictive. I couldn't believe I was actually talking to one of the men whom molested me it came from out of nowhere. I tried to reach out to each one of my molesters. I contacted some of their family members and I looked them up on inmate.com. I sent Maurice "Munk" Moody a copy of my book along with my number.

One of Antonio's cousins inboxed me his information in jail. I posted on Facebook I could not locate which prison Antonio was

Maurice "Munk" Moody — Child Molester

in. I sent Antonio "Coop" Davis a copy of my book along with my number. Maurice and Antonio were both incarcerated I listed my PO Box as my return address. Michael Moore whom is Antonio's brother is deceased along with Alex McKenny.

One of my girls from the hood told Greg "Double G" Conwell about the book. I reached out to his wife on Facebook and told her about my books and who I was. She read my message but never replied.

Greg's daughter reached out to me on messenger and asked, "Why are you saying these things about my father?"

I replied and told her, "Your father did indeed molest me when I was a child. Your father made me perform oral sex on him and this is a way of me receiving justice by letting the world know what he did, being that my Statute of Limitations has expired!"

She replied back and said, "My daddy said that you're lying."

I replied, "Well tell your dad to sue me then!!!!"

Anthony "Big Ant" Magee's twin sister reached out to me and asked about what I post on Facebook. She already knew about my book *Eyes Without A Face* when it was first released. I posted on Facebook about Anthony having sex with me without a condom under one of his pictures I put on Facebook. I told her it was true, I told her about his penis, that it was uncut and smelly and he had rough sex with me. She had nothing else to say.

Stacy Ray Whitt was the main one I was after. I found out he had other victims. I wanted his ass arrested ASAP! August 2015, I posted pictures of all of the men who molested me on Facebook again. That weekend, I finally got what I was looking for as more victims came forward stating Stacy either molested or raped them. It was all women. There were 10 to be exact. That meant this motherfucker had a total of 11 victims! I was livid and hurt. I felt bad

Anthony "Big Ant" Magee — Child Molester

for everyone. All I could think about was how their lives had been changed over the years.

Everyone had, if not the same story, similar stories. Stacy raped a total of five women molested five women and also molested me. This was unbelievable! I felt like a lawyer taking down everyone's information. Within a matter of three days back to back all 10 women came forward. The relationships the victims had between Stacy and them was what blew me away.

All of these women came forward one after another August 9, 2015, 4 women came forward, his niece was the first to come on this day. The next day, August 10th one of Stacy's baby mothers came forward and his niece's cousin. On August 11, three women who lived in the Color Doors (St. John Homes apartments) at the time they were raped came forward.

Stacy even raped one of his baby mothers. Stacy was caught having sex with his own niece whom was not even older than nine years old and fondled that niece's cousin. Stacy raped two other women at gun point, drugged three women whom were all friends that lived in the Color Doors apartments, molested two of his baby mothers' daughters and molested me.

Why Did We Meet? — It Wasn't' By Choice

*Stayla "Stacy Ray" Whitt — Child Molester & Rapist.
Has 11 victims total so far.*

Stacy's timeline when he first started his horrific sadistic events began in 1989. It could have begun before that but this was the information I gathered from the victims that came forward. It saddens me Gary, Indiana police has to have four victims come forward to make an arrest and extradition. I pray the two victims who have not filed charges come forward to receive their justice. I thank

TIMELINE

- From 1989 to 1995 Stacy Ray Whitt molested his niece he penetrated her she was only 4 years old when he first began. It last until she was 10 years old she is scared to file charges and will be 31 years old December 2016. Her Statue of Limitations will expire if she does not file charges by then.
- During the same time Stacy Ray Whitt fondled his niece's older cousin who pressed charges against him. She committed suicide by drug overdose August 2016.
- In 1990, Stacy Ray Whitt raped Lisa Ellis.
- In 1991, Stacy Ray Whitt molested me.
- From 1993 to 1998, Stacy Ray Whitt raped his baby mother and molested her daughter and her daughter pressed charges.
- In 1997, Stacy Ray Whitt raped female Jay at gunpoint.
- In 1999, Stacy Ray Whitt drugged and raped three females one female he raped he also molested her daughter after he raped her. They went to the hospital because they both had vaginal tears the female's daughter was only two years old. All three victims lived in the Color Doors apartments (St. John Homes).
- From 2001 to 2005, Stacy Ray Whitt molested another one of his baby mother's children she was only six years old when he started molesting her it lasted until she was 10 years old. Her mother told her to "Let it go, it happened and you didn't tell anyone then so do not bring his name up ever again in this house!" She also told her she could not file charges!
- Because of all these victims coming forward I made it my business to keep posting my molesters pictures I know more people would come forward. I felt dedicated to the cause, my mission was to help anyone who had been abused, bullied or mistreated in any manner. ENOUGH IS ENOUGH!

the two who did press charges; they have spoken up for the remaining ones that can't press charges because our Statute of Limitations has expired.

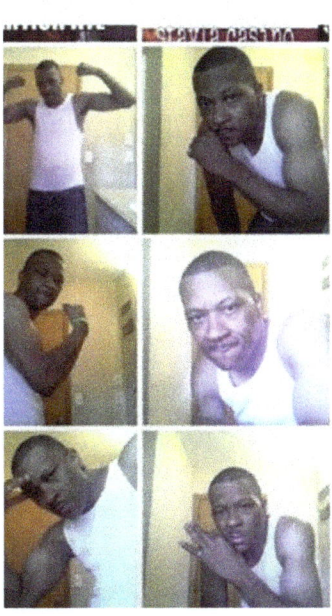

* * * * *

I sent all the ladies who were molested or raped by Stacy Ray Whitt a group text message, asking them if they felt comfortable writing their stories and sending them to me. I wanted to list their stories so people could see how they had become one of Stacy Ray Whitt's victims. I sent them the entire text message in a group message so they could see they were not alone and so they would be able to converse. Sometimes you have to hear from someone who walked in your shoes.

I felt they needed to see their own stories so they could understand how deep their pain is rooted. I also wanted them to be able to read the stories of the other victims. I was hoping by reading others stories it would give the young ladies who hadn't press charges the courage to press charges. Sometimes when you see others have endured your pain and by the same hands it may make you want to seek justice.

*** Stop being a prisoner of pain, speak up because you're hurting no one but yourself when is your time to heal?! If not now then when?! ***

THEIR STORIES IN THEIR OWN WORDS
Hear from "Stacy Ray Whitt" Victims
In the order of who how I received the stories...

VICTIM #6: HIS NIECE

I remember when he first moved in with us. I never thought things would go the way they did. It started with us watching late night movies while everyone was asleep. I would pretend like I was sleep until everyone else went to sleep. He would wait up for me. He would always have snacks for me and let me watch whatever I wanted. I didn't see anything wrong with it or worth telling because in my eyes he was the cool uncle.

Then one night after my mom had a long party & I actually fall asleep, I remember him waking me up with his hands over my mouth. Not too tight, just enough so I knew to be quiet. He grabbed my hand & led me to the living room. This night he let me sit on his lap while he rubbed my hair, then my ears, & then my neck. I remember him whispering in ear but I couldn't understand what he was saying. I then felt something wet on my ear because he kissing on it.

I pushed backed & turned around & he stuck his tongue down my throat. I tried to push him off but I wasn't strong enough. He told me it was our little secret and if I wanted to continue having our special movie nights I would keep it that way. If I would have known what I do now "our special movie nights would have ended."

So, we continued to have our late night meet ups, but nothing else accord for a while. Until one night my mom wasn't home and he woke me up. He kissed me again, only this time I didn't fight. I guess he felt as if I was ready and sent me to bathroom. I said I needed to brush my teeth before I went to because I had just eaten some candy. So, I did just that.

I heard a knock on the bathroom door and I opened it. Before I could open the door all the way he rushed in. He sat on the toilet. He put his head on my stomach and started crying. I asked him what was wrong & he didn't say anything. I asked him did he hurt and he said yes. I asked where — something I regret. He pulled out his penis & told me if I rubbed it he would feel better. I'm a six-year-old girl whose parents never talked to her about sex.

I mean why would they. I was only six. So, of course I rubbed it in hopes of making him feel better. Judging from the look on his face, he felt better. He kissed me on the forehead and said GN.

Maybe about a month later while watching TV and he was drunk he woke up and grabbed my private. I was confused. I don't know what to do. He crawled on the floor with me and put some cover over us. He started kissing me all over my body. Then he asked me to sit on the couch with him. He sat me on his lap.

I remember feeling him messing with his pants. I didn't know what was about to happen. He pulled my panties to the side & pushed his penis in. I jumped up QUICKLY. I remember it hurting like hell. He told me to be his big girl & take it. He gently sat me back down but this time he eased it in and he didn't put it all in.

I remember crying and him holding my mouth. Him whispering in my ear, "You're too loud and if you're mom and Darryl wake up movie night would be over; be my big girl it's almost over."

I didn't know what he was talking about. I thought he meant the pain was almost over. But in all actuality the pain had just begun. Once he was done that night, I didn't want movie night anymore. But he told me that if I said anything he would get in trouble for having movie night with me and I would too for sneaking out my room.

So, with me afraid to get in trouble he felt more comfortable. He rubs, grab, or lick me whenever wherever. Whenever he felt he had the opportunity he took it.

My mom had to notice a change in me because, she would ask what was wrong and I would look at him and say nothing. Although the sex wasn't going on anymore at that moment he still would do other things.

Then one night I remember him telling me he miss that feeling I gave him, he missed our movie nights, he missed being with me and he loved me. He apologized for hurting me and told me I'm the only one that can make him feel that way and I should feel special because I'm a kid doing what most grown women can't do. (Whatever that meant.)

He told me I was special and to just give him another chance. He promised me it wouldn't hurt like the last time and he'll do whatever I wanted him to do. He'll keep me out of trouble and make sure no one messes with me.

I asked him would he really do that for me and he said yes, "that's what boyfriends do for their girlfriends." Of course I went for it and we ended up kissing. He actually showed me how to kiss properly that night. He laid me on my back and slowly pushed his dick inside me. It was hurting, so I screamed. He stuck his tongue in my mouth and said, "Hush you're a woman now."

I tried my best to muffle my screams. I admit it didn't hurt as much as the last time but it still hurt. So, from that point on in my mind I felt as if we were a couple and what we were doing was OK because he Loved Me!

* * * * *

In the midst of the victims coming forward, a man also came forward. This is a conversation with someone from FB. He was around 18 or 19 years old when he was dealing with Stacy Ray Whitt.

13/08/2015 23:05 **ANONYMOUS**

Whatz good sir I did not realize that I knew Stacy until just the other day. I never knew he did all that...to you and others. I am praying for that brother

12/08/2015 13:05 **Author Samuel Holloway III**

Thank you so much for your support

13/08/2015 23:05 **ANONYMOUS**

I know this dude he does mess around trust me. I dealt with him many many years ago

12/08/2015 13:05 **Author Samuel Holloway III**

WHAT?!!

13/08/2015 23:05 **ANONYMOUS**

Yeah just between me and you and u don't wanna go on record about a thing...he use to live with his baby mom and he use to beat the hell outta her. I think I was like 18 or 19. I lived on 21 and Carolina and he lived like off 21st Street.

Please don't put my name out there

12/08/2015 13:05 **Author Samuel Holloway III**

I don't do that bro. Everyone is confidential unless they tell me it's ok. I am interested in the story thou

13/08/2015 23:05 **ANONYMOUS**

I mate at the gas station on 21st and he asked to use my phone. We dealt for a while nothing to sirerous. He liked head. But he had a girlfriend and was cheating on her

The gas station around the street from Saints Home church

12/08/2015 13:05 *Author Samuel Holloway III*

Damn!! I know exactly where that is. I know the girl he was with at the time because of the timeline of the victims

13/08/2015 23:05 **ANONYMOUS**

I think he lived like on Louisiana in a small house

12/08/2015 13:05 *Author Samuel Holloway III*

Yea he did

13/08/2015 23:05 **ANONYMOUS**

This was like 1996 because that was my 1st apartment. Or 1997. So you know I'm not lieing

12/08/2015 13:05 *Author Samuel Holloway III*

Yep we think he left Gary 10 yrs later. Oh I def believe u

13/08/2015 23:05 **ANONYMOUS**

He almost got caught by the police e in my car behind the career center

12/08/2015 13:05 *Author Samuel Holloway III*

Do u know he if went to jail or caught a charge

13/08/2015 23:05 **ANONYMOUS**

No we almost got caught. No jail for me.

12/08/2015 13:05 **Author Samuel Holloway III**

Oh ok

13/08/2015 23:05 **ANONYMOUS**

I stop dealing with him because he was to much to aggressive and a drunk. And that girl called my phone and I told her what was going on and he beat the hell outta her

12/08/2015 13:05 **Author Samuel Holloway III**

Damn.... Everybody say the aggressive thing. OMG was her name Donita

13/08/2015 23:05 **ANONYMOUS**

I think so she had a bunch of kids

12/08/2015 13:05 **Author Samuel Holloway III**

OMG... Did u see her

13/08/2015 23:05 **ANONYMOUS**

She came outside once and he cussed her out and we drove off. So when he said he like pussy that's a lie he like boys.

12/08/2015 13:05 **Author Samuel Holloway III**

Please describe what u remember as far as what she looks like. I said that I promise.

13/08/2015 23:05 **ANONYMOUS**

Truth be told I don't remember I was young he I thought he was so fine and a nigga only to find out now he is child molester

Was sorry

12/08/2015 13:05 **Author Samuel Holloway III**

Right bro right

13/08/2015 23:05 **ANONYMOUS**

I hope he fo to jail and they rip his ass whole out

*12/08/2015 13:05 **Author Samuel Holloway III***

I do too! And I'm going to write him everyday! ☺

13/08/2015 23:05 **ANONYMOUS**

I wanna tell him he should just come clean and say he like boys
I'm there are more boys in that area over there that he has fucked with

*12/08/2015 13:05 **Author Samuel Holloway III***

You don't have too! I could just post ur messages! Your name won't be in them then he would know!

OMG OMG please let me post this!

13/08/2015 23:05 **ANONYMOUS**

Ok as long as my name does not come up...I am not a shame of who I am but I a Minister in my church and have a partner of 9 years

*12/08/2015 13:05 **Author Samuel Holloway III***

I got you bro! You will see what I'm about to post now

13/08/2015 23:05 **ANONYMOUS**

I mean I am openly gay but keep my life outside of fb
Ok

*12/08/2015 13:05 **Author Samuel Holloway III***

I understand

13/08/2015 23:05 **ANONYMOUS**

Ok

* * * * *

VICTIM #5: STACY RAPED HER AT GUNPOINT

Stacy and I worked at "Per Pak" warehouse together and we were dating for about 2 or 3 weeks. He seemed to be cool so I invited him over. He tried to have sex with me and I told him no, we didn't know each other well enough.

It was like he snapped and became cold. He raped me with my two-year-old son in the next room. I cried and he said to me, "You one of them crying bitches," and continued to rape me. The next day at work he acted like nothing happened and he said to me, "That shit too good for you to be keeping it to yourself but next time I'm going let you give it to me."

* * * * *

VICTIM #9: STACY WHITT DRUGGED AND RAPED HER.

The fact is that I had a crush on Stacy. I enjoyed his company and him being around me so I'll let him come over and we will chill n chat but one day we were drinking and he kept refilling my cup and I blanked out and I woke up at 5 a.m. he was gone my shorts and underwear were off and I had a wet ass.

I felt violated and confused wondering exactly what happened and if he let someone else rape me too. It still affects me to this day because I want know what happened that night. I tried to reach out to him recently and he denied even chilling with me and even blocked me on Facebook so I'll never know what happened.

* * * * *

My last death threat to date came from Shavon Missy Jones and Victor Young AKA Lil Vic. Lil Vic is from the hood of 22nd Ave and grew up with my brother. Lil Vic was actually my brother's cousin,

cousin on his dad's side. Missy was from Delaney projects in Gary they have a special relationship from back in the day when we were teenagers. I never knew Missy personally and she didn't know me.

Missy tried to set me up to be killed by Lil Vic! August of 2015 Missy contacted me on the Facebook messenger app, her initial inquiries were about my books and pictures of the men who molested me. Missy wanted to get a couple of copies of my books for her sister and herself. By this time both books "Eyes Without A Face" and "How It All Happened" were out. She told me she knew some of the people in my books I listed in the "DL MEN" chapter. Missy stated she had grown up with some of the men too and gave me her number to call.

I was posting on Facebook looking for pictures of the men that molested me I wanted to put the name with the face and post their pictures. I already post pictures of Maurice "Munk" Moody, Stacy Ray Whitt, Anthony Magee and Alex McKenny who is deceased. I needed pictures of Greg "Double G" Conwell, Antonio Davis and Michael Moore Antonio's younger brother who is also deceased.

When I called Missy she sounded happy. Immediately the first question she asked after telling me she was from the hood in GI (Gary) was "What part of Atlanta I lived in." Before I could answer, Missy stated she lived in Riverdale but was at her daughter's job at the time. I told her I lived in Atlanta. She went on to say how long she's been living here in Georgia and she really needed to connect with me.

Missy stated she had gone through so much growing up and she could relate to my books. Missy said Lil Vic, Ty, her home girl and herself went to a hotel off Cline Ave back in the day. She said they were all cool and went to the hotel to smoke and drink. Missy stated her girl and Ty were having sex on one bed while she and

Why Did We Meet? — It Wasn't' By Choice

Greg "Double G" Conwell — Child Molester

Lil Vic were on the other bed. Missy said she passed out and woke up lying next to Lil Vic but she was naked and Lil Vic drugged and raped her and she never reported it.

As I listened to her I was writing down everything she was saying. I was in shock I know Lil Vic is a scandalous person but I didn't know he was a rapist too. He served almost twelve years total for a series of things from drugs, guns and murder charges in prison. Missy went on to say she had pictures of Antonio and Greg on her page, and that was what I really wanted to hear. I began to ask where the pictures on her page were she took a thousand selfies a day, she directed me to the exact folder.

I was going through the folder and telling her what pictures I was seeing to see was I close to their pictures. Missy took the conversation right back to where I lived in Atlanta. Missy said, "So what are you by in Atlanta like what street you live on or what's by you?" Again while hurrying through her pictures I said, "I live in Atlanta right in the heart of the city" when I said that I stumbled across Greg "Double G" Conwell picture. With my heart racing I snapshot the picture with my phone. I told her after I snapshot the picture I found Greg's picture and quickly asked where was Antonio's and Michael's picture.

Again Missy took the conversation back to where I lived. This time I said Midtown but I don't see the other 2 pictures. Missy said she was tagged in the pictures from Nettie (Antonio and Michael's sister) and Nettie must have deleted the pictures. Then said, "well I'm about to leave my daughter's job so if you want I can come pick up the books right now!" I felt something in my spirit wasn't right and told her I was at school at the moment and when I got out of class I would call her. She said cool and we hung up.

Immediately I called 2 of my home girls who lives in Gary. Both of them said the same exact thing to me, "Be careful because she is either Lil Vic's girlfriend or they are just fucking!" They both told me to go on Lil Vic's page and through his pictures. I went through Lil Vic's page and was pissed off. This bitch was everywhere on his page. They had many pictures together. I blew off the fact she was trying to get my address because I didn't give it to her and Lil Vic was in jail but I did get a picture I was looking for and I let it go.

Not even 4 months later Lil Vic was released from jail. He threatened me on Facebook and said, "I am going to put a bullet in your head!" Of course I went straight to the police I am not a fighter but I will fight. Posting on any social media site you are going to kill anyone is considered a "Terroristic Threat." After I filed the police report I made a couple more calls to Gary I needed his probation officer number being he was on probation. Within 3 days Lil Vic was arrested but not for the Terroristic Threat, he was arrested for selling cocaine to an undercover police officer and served 1 year in jail. Karma is a bitch!

Lil Vic was released from jail in late October early November. I was contacted by Danny my best friend Angela's ex-boyfriend. Danny hated Lil Vic, they fought back in the day and Lil Vic and another person jumped Danny. Danny called and told me Lil Vic got released from jail and was living here in Atlanta with Shavon Missy Jones. I was livid! I was beyond pissed off I screamed out loud "This bitch tried to set me up!" I was so mad I was crying!

Without any hesitation I went straight to Facebook and posted…

ME: *I am furious right now. So this bitch Shavon Missy Jones tried to set me up! She was in my inbox asking for 2 copies of my books for her sister and her, gave me some pictures of the men pictures that I had been for and gave me her number to call. All the while, this bitch has the nicca living with her that Threatened to kill me on Facebook.*

Missy: *Tell me where you see set up. If I wanted know where u lived I can look up in a medical database whatever you and homeboy got going on that between you. But if this to get your book sale up… Do you boo boo*

Missy: *Not crazy homeboy take everything out context. Cuz.. He piss with Lil Vic go after him.*

ME: *No bitch, I don't take shit out of content. What the fuck you needed my address for when you could have just ordered off line?! I know*

Missy: *FYI you said meet me by my gig Boo boo Dekalb never need your address. But if u like to say what u got to say in my face shoot that address to me now cause Facebook Gangsta is not my style homeboy...*

Danny: *O SO PEOPLE DON'T THINK PEOPLE FUCK WITH ME IN GARY HUH...WELL AUTHOR SAMUEL HOLLOWAY III SINCE MISSY AND LIL VICK WANNA PLAY WITH YOUR LIFE U CAN PLAY WITH THEIR LIFE BEST FRIEND (with a bunch of laughing emoji faces) I HAVE THE ADDRESS TO WHERE THEY LIVE...I TOLD YALL THEY STAY IN AN APARTMENT...IM GOOD AT WHAT I DO IF I WANT U I CAN FIND U (with the eye emoijis and laughing faces) ONE WAY OR ANOTHER HERE U GO SAM LETS PLAY THEIR GAME...269 HIGHWAY 138 SW APT 2202 RIVERDALE GEORGIA 30274 4070 (with a bunch of laughing emoji faces)*

Before I could reply to Danny's post of Missy's address, Danny tagged me and 49 other people in the post.

Right after Danny posted Missy's address, she was furious. She posted on Facebook that this wasn't right and she was calling the police. I was thinking to myself, *Bitch, are you serious? You basically gave my address away on Facebook and now you want to call the police? Bitch Really??!!! Where they do that at??!!* Apparently right here in ATL.

Needless to say, Missy called her brother who is a security guard for some apartments here in Atlanta and made a video. She stated they don't play any games when it comes to fuckery and they will deal with the situation. By the next morning, all of Missy's posts were deleted, including the video and she unfriended me, too. Bye, Bitch!

Everybody knows I'm no dummy and I'm not a Facebook gangster. I was making my calls to the police station! I'd rather take your freedom away before I do something that I will regret and can't take back. Jonesboro Police Department told me to file a police report in the city where I lived because the threat took place on Facebook. I called my police department in my city and they took the police report. After the police officer was done taking my report he suggested I file a "Temporary Protective Order" after looking at Victor Young's rap sheet. He stated, "Victor Young seems like a dangerous person and it's better to be safe than sorry."

I did just that and filed a "Temporary Protective Order" in Jonesboro and had them served. I knew if Lil Vic was here in Atlanta it was definitely not for a good thing or to become a better person. Lil Vic moved here strictly on the account of killing me! I post on Facebook about him asking me for money and giving him head. I also post the screen shot of him telling me he loved me. This was the same person who hated me growing up. This was also the same person that tried to jump me along with his homeboy, not to mention this is the same person who shot a bullet through my ex-best friend Michial's mom's car window because he hated gay men so badly. But now he was telling me he loved me on Facebook messenger and in about every letter he's written me while he was in jail. He always talked about how I left a good nicca for these lame niccas and what he could do for me sexually!

Almost a month later April 8, 2016 was our court date. I was going to court for a "Temporary Protective Order" against Lil Vic and Missy. My boyfriend Clinton and my home girl Diane went to court with me. We took 2 cars in case they were waiting in the parking lot and arrived a little early before the scheduled time. I didn't want them to get my tag from my car. Diane and I went into the court building while Clinton sat in the car waiting behind looking to see what they would pull up in. He had screen shot their pictures so he knew what they looked like.

As it got closer to 8:30am, the time court was to be in session, I called and told Clinton to come in because neither of them had showed up yet. We entered the court room and the guard sat people according to how they filed or had charges filed against them. I sat to the left, the people who didn't file but were there with others sat in the middle and the people who had charges filed against them sat to the right. Missy or Lil Vic never showed up and the judge dismissed the case until they could be served he stated they had not been served.

I was pissed. I knew some people hated me so much they wanted me dead, now I had a total of thirteen death threats! This death threat did have me scared and I felt threatened and found myself looking over my shoulder for a couple of days. I learned sometimes you take a loss. I had to lift that spirit off me by praying, "No weapon formed against me shall prosper!" People only try to kill the truth but will let a lie run like a forest fire.

I was very lost on the death threats. Why hadn't anyone sent Lil Vic any death threats? After all, Lil Vic made the "Hammond Times" newspaper but many men from the hood didn't know because they don't like to read or don't know how. Lil Vic can't be trusted! He's a snitch! He's been a snitch for the last 13 years right under everyone's nose! Someone who sold crack to their own mother and testified against their own brother can never be trusted! The article posted on May 15, 2002 states.

JUDGE SENTENCES 'LITTLE VIC' FOR DRUG POSSESSION

HAMMOND — U.S. District Court Judge James T. Moody sentenced the leader of a notorious Gary street gang to nine years in prison Tuesday.

The sentence represents a break for Victor "Little Vic" Young, 24, of Gary, who was a high-ranking figure in the 22nd Avenue Boys, a faction of the nationwide Vice Lords street gang in the early 1990s.

Moody agreed to lower his sentence in return for his cooperation with federal authorities who have sent 13 other members of the gang to prison for drug dealing and violence that has contributed to Gary's high homicide rate.

Young's brother, Terrence "Jack" Young, is serving a 65-year prison term for selling cocaine, marijuana and directing a campaign of drive-by shootings against rival gang members.

The Young brothers' gang draws its name from its turf near 22nd Avenue and Broadway in Gary where it operated a series of drug houses. The U.S. attorney's office said that whenever Gary police would raid and close down one house, the gang would resume business in another down the street.

Victor Young was himself a victim of a shooting during the 1994 Taste of Gary melee where rival gangs shot it out among carnival-goers at a summer festival sponsored by the city.

Police said Young was suspected of involvement in other drug and violent crimes, but had trouble finding enough evidence and credible witnesses to make any charges stick until his arrest on federal charges of possession of crack cocaine July 19, 1996.

He pleaded guilty to that charge last January under an agreement in which he will continue to cooperate in future prosecutions of gang members.

• •

One day Miyasha and I were chatting like we always did and she said this *"Our problem started from back then think about this. Back in slavery a man had to watch his wife get raped. He couldn't SAY anything he couldn't protect her and he couldn't do anything! Subconsciously throughout the years generation after generation we can't be surprised after all these years that people are still silent about being touched or different things going on in the households and that has messed us up mentally. Until we can take care of the shit in house the generational curse is going to continue the longer this goes on the harder it will be to break the cycle."*

I am not what happened to me. I am what I choose to become dealing with my past and helping others with theirs sparked passion in my soul. I want to help as many people as possible while helping myself too. I can't do this alone there are so many people in this world hurting from abuse but feel nothing can be done. Most times if they want to press charges they can't because their "Statue of Limitations" has expired. I started a petition called "Sam's Law" it will help those individuals affected have justice. "Sam's Law" will extend the "Statue of Limitations" for an extra 10 years. There should never be a time limit on seeking justice from someone who abused anyone by molestation, rape, abuse or sexual abuse. Enough Is Enough!

Some people always say, "You can't do anything about your past so stop talking about it." That's lie! I can do something about my past and I am! I am going to STOP THE LAW OF LIMITATIONS! If this law were NOT in existence I wouldn't have the problem of pressing charges.

We need to stand together to help someone, remember this could be someone you know you're helping by signing the petition because this could even be for you. We all live in this world together I know we all have our beliefs and things we partake in but this right here needs your full undivided attention. This petition needs to go viral! PLEASE, I ask you NOT to look at the person making this petition but look at the children, teens, young adults and adults this petition will help seek justice. What if this were you trying to seek justice from someone who took your child hood, abused or raped you, or a family member.

How far would you go to seek justice?? Many of us can't because of the "Statue of Limitation." This law only gives 10 years to press charges. Most people who were victimized wait until after the 10 year mark and our justice is gone forever. Let's make "Sam's Law" legal by extending the "Statue of Limitation" law! PLEASE sign this petition so we can make that happen. It does take a village to raise a child!

The petition is found at:

https://www.change.org/p/the-public-Facebook-twitter-global-14-tagged-instagram-sign-this-petition-to-take-the-statute-of-limitations-away-for-people-who-were-molested-abused-and-or-raped?utm_campaign=petition_lonely&utm_medium=email&utm_source=guides

I put my life on the line for your child like my mother should have put her life on the line for me! Don't be my mother and don't let your child be me! Sometimes when I pray at night I pray for my enemies and my molesters because if this were them they would not know what to do.

A lot of people wanted me to release the names of the men I knew were on the "Down Low." I was close to doing it then I thought about all the women who were hurting because of these men living a double life. I thought about the families that would be ruined. This was totally different than releasing the names of the men who molested me. These men had not done anything to me. I just knew some of them were complete liars! I thought about how these same men from Gary degraded gay men in front of their friends, family and mates. These men painted a horrible picture of gay men to others, all the while having sex and receiving head from them.

It was simply the overplay for the underlay, they didn't want anyone to suspect they were "Down Low Men" they basically made sure others hated gay men, too. After careful consideration I decided to only release a few names of the men who are "Down Low." This is not part of my mission and I don't want the men listed as "Down Low" to overshadow my message. Everyone already knew about Mikey D and Lil Bob.

However, my loyalty is with those who kept their loyalty to me. Cedric didn't check his baby momma nor did he check his cousin. His baby mommy kept asking me in my inbox on Facebook about Cedric and I. She became rude after I told her to talk to him after she asked me a few times already if he and I had messed around. She kept replying back saying she had spoken to him and he kept telling her that we didn't mess around. I'm just lost why some women are so lost. If I told you my loyalty is with him basically I'm confirming your thoughts without saying yes, why would you ask him and then ask me again and again.

I'm thinking she had to be fighting with the belief of knowing her baby daddy was with me before her. I loved Cedric! He was my first real "DL" love. We were young he was eighteen and I was twenty. In my mind I dated Cedric for a total of three years. We never had sex it was just oral relations. He was dating my home girl when we first started conversing on that level.

I know she suspected something because Cedric and I were a little too close for comfort. I started being her friend once I knew he wanted to talk her. My ex best friend Michial was already her friend. After a while I moved to Minnesota and he stayed in Gary. My cousin Nina and I would go back and forth to Gary every other weekend just so I could see him.

Nina worked at the Mall of America and I would go "shopping for free" for Cedric and me. On two occasions, I got us matching outfits along with my cousin/brother Troy and his girlfriend to take pictures in. Troy and Cedric were best friends, everyone including my close friends and family knew about us. Although Cedric had a girlfriend, I didn't care because I knew he wasn't going to be with me. He was straight with a little twist and I was living in the moment. She knew I liked him and she never questioned our relationship so I didn't bother to tell her. I was young and "turning out as many straight men" as I could.

As long as they don't cross me their secret life is safe with me and I will forever be "Loyal" to them. I hope people start to pay attention and stop thinking because a man acts hard, has children, is a thug or had sex with many women that that makes a man straight, definitely that's not the case!

I began talking more about "DL Men" and sharing pictures of the men who molested me. There were over 585 likes, 565 shares, 704 comments by the end of the night, the wheels were turning now. May 6, 2016 I found out one of my molesters was working around children I was livid! Anthony Magee was working at a fitness center in Gary and he wasn't even working out, Anthony is a big guy. I had no doubt in my heart he got the job to work near children and teenagers. I did what anyone would do who has been molested and found out their abuser works around children, I called his job!

On the first attempt trying to reach the Director he didn't want to talk with me he felt I was recording the conversation. I called Anthony's job earlier the same day and recorded the call and put it on Facebook and tagged his job within the post. The Director was not in at the time and I was told to call back, I also asked for Anthony but he was off work. When I called back and spoke to the Director he informed me he viewed the video posted and didn't want to have a conversation with me because he felt I was recording the call. I told him I wasn't recording the call but I didn't call there so he could have a conversation with me, I called to have a conversation with him and he needed to listen.

After a few hours the superintendent sent me a message on Facebook asking me to give her a call. I called her back and explained to her I was not trying to be vindictive or doing this out of spite. I needed to inform her there was a child molester working for their company and they needed to be aware and talk to the children in case Anthony got to any of them. She told me she and management would give me a call on Monday and it would be a conference call. She stated in the meantime if I could find anyone that may have felt uncomfortable around Anthony to write a letter and they could remain anonymous.

Immediately I posted a message on Facebook that read:

"I've spoken with someone from the Gary Parks Department concerning Anthony Magee, the man who molested me when I was 12 years old! Please listen — If your child attends Hudson Campbell Sports & Fitness Center please talk to your child. Ask them questions. Let's not forget Stacy Whitt had 10 other victims. A child molester does not stop!

Ask your child if they've come in contact with Anthony Magee. Ask them if he has touched them inappropriately, followed them or made them feel uncomfortable. Please inbox me because we need to hear from you! You can remain anonymous.

Please don't sweep this prevalent issue concerning our youth under the rug!"

On May 9, 2016 I had the conference call with the fitness center's management team. On the call was the Director, someone from the Human Resource department, the Superintendent and the Chief of Staff. I knew more than likely they were recording the call and taking notes just like I was. The lady from Human Resources did the majority of the talking. First she asked me to explain the situation, I began by telling her I am the author of two books, *Eyes Without A Face* and *How It All Happened*, which details my life and about how seven men molested me whom were my brother's friends.

I told her I never pressed charges at the time I was a 12 year old child. I told her I didn't tell my mother because I didn't have that type of support. I told her I used all of my molester's real names within my books which came out four years, four months, and six days prior to calling the fitness center. I informed her soon as I found out Anthony Magee worked for them I immediately called there to inform them they had a grown man who molested me when I was a child working around children and I wanted to make sure they were aware of him and his actions.

I then told her when I spoke with the Superintendent on Friday and while waiting for this call she stated they did a complete background check on Anthony Magee and his background was clean. I told her they need to run another background check because Anthony was just released from prison not jail a couple of years prior. I told them they may need to check his social security number, date of birth or the way he spelled his name because his background is not clean!

After that the superintendent asked, did any parents reach out to me concerning Anthony Magee. I told her yes and she asked me to email her whatever I had and did I have the information on my phone. I told her yes and she texted me and said to text everything back to the number. After that the Human Resource lady said they would do an investigation and get back to me, and then we ended the call. They never called me back and he still works there!

Oh, how I can't wait for my day of justice, I know it's coming this is not revenge this is seeking justice by any means necessary! Unfortunately some people think what I'm doing is negative however picture a child being touched by an adult inappropriately. I didn't want any of my molesters around children and if I can stop it I will! What would you do?'

When I finally had the chance to speak to Anthony Magee, the man whom molested me at 12 years old, this is what he had to say to me...

Phone rings
Female answers: "Hello, thanks for calling (Job name). How can I help you?"
Me: May I speak with Anthony Magee?
Her: Hold on....(screams out, "Anthony, telephone!")
Anthony: Hello?
Me: What's good, bro?
Anthony: Nothing much. Who this?
Me: This Romie's little brother, Robert!
Anthony: Who?
Me: This Romie's little brother, Robert. (My name was Robert at that time.)
Anthony: Ok. What's up?!
Me: Just checking on you!
Anthony: Why are you calling my job?!
Me: Because I want to!

Anthony put the phone down and never returned!

I recorded myself calling Anthony Magee's job and then posted the video next to his picture on Facebook. This is how it read...

I called Anthony Magee's job last week. I just hung up because I realized he was no longer coming back to the phone after he laid it down. He remembers me! He remembers what he did too!

It took me a couple of days to post this. I had to gather my thoughts. I'm hated because I'm speaking my truth! People tell me to stop posting about my past and so many other negative things.

However, these same people don't even know the person the way that I know them.

This mission is so no other child will have my story! I'm going to make sure that everyone knows everyone that I listed the way I know them!

It took me this long to post it because it was the holiday and I was traveling and I didn't want this to overshadow my trip and I didn't want this to get overlooked!

I wanted to just snap the fuck out but I knew I had to play cool when dealing with these men! Manipulate the manipulator! I'm coming!

SHARE TAG PLEASE

* * * * *

After I posted the video of Anthony Magee, 3 victims came forward. One stated Anthony raped her, another stated Anthony tried to rape her and the last stated Anthony tried to molest her when she was a child. One of Anthony Magee victims said her rape occurred at "N-Effect" night club located in Gary. She did go to the hospital and have a rape kit done afterward but didn't report it because she was afraid of what her parents would think of her, they belonged to a well-known church. As far as my other molesters only 1 stated she was raped by Alex McKenny who is deceased.

VICTIM #1...

Anthony raped me in 1996 at N Effect Club in Gary. I did a rape kit in Hammond but only told my best friend. My parents are very religious. I could only think of what they would think of me. I never reported it and I was 18 at the time. I'm glad you posted that picture of Anthony. We all went to Wirt School together. I'm so thankful you posted his picture! I thought I was the only one.

VICTIM # 2...

I don't remember his name but his face, the fat one with the hair cut, dark skin, the one job you called. My parents were drug addicts when I was growing up in Dorie Miller projects and they let people sell drugs out our home so our house was a spot.

So a bunch of people was over chilling doing what grown folks do and I was up in my room asleep. I heard my door open and someone come in and close the door so I stayed pretending like I was sleep.

I watched what he was doing for a minute. He walked to the window looked out of it maybe twice and then came over to me and tried to pull down my shorts and panties but I got up. I couldn't let it go any further. I was only ten and was scared and a virgin.

I told my mom but she was in the room getting high at the time so she kind of blew it off. And the guy was trying to say I was lying was (K.R.) his friend but why would I. No one was in my room but me and dude.

VICTIM 3...

I was born & raised in Gary, IN. In Aetna — i was in the 7th grade (4sure) when this happened!!! Ant always let me know he was interested — being the popular guy/ladies man that he was I think I felt some type of special when I was invited 2 his home – upon arrival he led me straight 2 his room & immediately tried ripn off my pants!!!

Not wanting 2 disrobe & being a virgin — I'm screaming no!!! Plz stop!!! & tryn 2 stop him!!! & he's super huge & I'm super skinny — there was no stopn him!!!

Thank u Jesus his mother was home & heard my tears!!! She busted in the room & said Anthony what are u doing??? I got up & quickly left with no plans 2 ever return!!!

Now I have kept this secret for years!!! I just told my husband not even a month ago & now I'm telln u!!!

It's another secret I have that I have buried until 2day!!! That secret also involves Anthony Magee!!! I had a friend that was a virgin before he raped her!!! When she shared her secret w/me I promised I'll never tell anyone & I feel so bad that I never shared my secret w/her!!! Just maybe if I told her what he tried 2 do 2 me I could've helped her thru the battle!!!

Soo Samuel Holloway, I believe every word of yo story, especially knowing my experience with that devil!!!

(Paragraphs and original all caps changed for readability.)

I've learned a lot throughout this whole ordeal you have to forgive people not because they need to be forgiven but because you need to be free! No matter what, I pray I can continue to have a caring, loving heart, despite what I've gone through. I hate no one and it takes a lot to be humble. There is so much knowledge out here and some people still choose to be ignorant.

CHAPTER 8

MY NEIGHBOR

The day before I was slated to graduate from college I saw this fine chocolate dude. Now everyone knows I am not attracted to chocolate men but this brother was PHINE with a capital P. OMG was he PHINE, he was everything, stood around 5'10", 180 pounds, solid, dread locks, big feet and big hands. **Side Smile**

He drove a muscle car, a silver 2012 Camaro with red stripes sitting on 22-inch rims. He was outside in my parking lot walking his pit-bull. We were just getting back from the mall shopping for outfits for the weekend parties lined up and last minute errands. I told Miyasha to ask him "what's his name his age where he stay and was he single." While getting things out of the trunk Miyasha called him over to us.

Miyasha said, "Hey you come here" she pointed her finger pulling him in. He approached us and I was staring at him up and down, I wanted him to see me looking so he knew I was interested. Everything worked like a charm, Miyasha started asking him questions which he answered with no problems while looking at me licking his lips. I was saying, *YYYYAAAASSSSSSSS!* in my mind.

Afterward, Miyasha said, "His ass is gay!" I asked her how did she know? Miyasha said, "Bitch, the entire time he was talking to me he was looking at you, smiling, and I'm fine as fuck!"

We all started laughing and Miyasha said, "Seriously, he was looking at you, smiling, when I'm the one who talking to him." Ole GAY ass!

His name was Tyrus, and he was 26 years old and a Sagittarius. He said his birthday was December 15 and I said, "Shut up" that's the same day as mine we really started staring at each other then. Miyasha went on to ask him more questions and he continued to answer them. He stayed right in the next building to mine which were connected, he was single and he just got off work. Tyrus was throwing more answers than Miyasha was asking questions and I was loving it.

After Miyasha was done interrogating Tyrus I said we needed to get a move on it, it was about 90-something degrees out. It had been hot all week and the forecast said the weather wasn't changing anytime soon. I extended my hand to Tyrus to shake his and he shook my hand and pulled me in for that brotherly hug. YES GAWD, I wanted to melt into his body, his body felt good in that wife beater, he had eggplant for days too in those basketball shorts. (Dick print) When we walked away I looked back to see him again I wanted to keep the vision in my mind for the night.

The next day later on that night after graduation I was making a weed run for Molly and Marilyn. I had just picked up Marilyn from the airport she flew in from New Orleans for my party she couldn't make my graduation. After I got everybody's weed I was coming back to the car I was leaving out the building of the weed man's house and Tyrus was walking up. I had the biggest smile I was happy to see him and I was shocked we used the same connect.

Tyrus gave me that brotherly hug again and asked what I had going on for the night. I told him I had friends in town and we were about to turn the city out. We laughed and he said put my number in your phone. Right before I locked his number in I said, "Your name Tyrus, right?"

He said, "Yessir and you're Trey. Right?"

I said, "Yessir!"

We both remembered each other's name — that was hot. **Blank Stare** We both went our separate ways.

After a couple of days passed I texted Tyrus late Friday night. I asked him if he wanted to match a blunt. Ya'll know weed is my unifier to men. He hit me back and said he already made plans but he would hit me up later if it wasn't too late I told him that would be cool. Sure enough later on around 2 a.m. Tyrus hit me up and asked was I awake. I wasn't but I texted him back and said yes. He asked what my apartment number was and he was outside in the parking lot. I gave him the address and he came up right away.

Tyrus knocked on the door, my heart was racing faster than speed racer. My dick was brick I just woke up and it didn't have any time to go down. Tyrus came in and I had to hide my dick I only had on boxer briefs and my print was out there. I turned around quickly and turned on the TV soon as he stepped in. He closed the door and locked it and came and shook my hand since I was sitting down. The living room was dark but the TV lit it up somewhat.

Tyrus asked should he take his shoes off and I said yes. He stood up and walked to the door while I stood up and headed to my room to put some basketball shorts on. I couldn't take it and I didn't want him to see me with a hard dick. I honestly didn't know if he was straight, gay, bi or curious, I had to play this safe. I came back in the living room and Tyrus had taken his shoes off as well as his shirt. He said, "Ay bro it's hot as hell in here" I turned on the fan and immediately thought "Good!" **Smiles Hard**

We smoked, watched TV and talked about life. Tyrus was real cool and we had a lot of similarities. We both shared the same birthday, were the youngest of our parent's children, single with no kids, have cars, lived alone and we loved to dress. Tyrus was sharp that night too. He had on some denim faded cut up jeans which showed his muscular thighs, a black and white wife beater with some type of design on it, some black Nike's and black ankle socks. His legs were to die for and they were not hairy, did I mention he was chocolate!

As the night went on we both started to doze off and Tyrus said he would hit me up tomorrow to do it again, we gave each other that brotherly hug and he left. The next morning Tyrus texted me around 8ish and asked did I want to come over and match a blunt. I was dead to the world but I got my ass up, brush my teeth and threw on some basketball shorts, a beater and ran out the door. I was moving so fast I forgot I didn't have his apartment number, I called him and he gave it to me.

I knocked on Tyrus' door and he yelled "Come in its open!" Chile when I walked through Tyrus door his ass was laid on the couch in nothing but his got damn boxers, I HOLLERED inside! I sat my ass down real quick next to him. He was lying down and I sat at his feet on the couch. His feet were so big and pretty they looked soft. He looked as if he just got done doing 300 pushups, his muscles were bulging and his nipples were hard. He lit his blunt and we started talking. I felt like a teenager in love with someone I had no clue about sexually. I didn't stare too hard I didn't want him to feel uncomfortable. He had a cover but he wasn't covered up, I realized "this bastard is teasing me!"

When we finished the blunts Tyrus got up from the couch and my eyes was glued to his eggplant, it was just swanging. He went to the bedroom and came back in basketball shorts and asked if I was hungry. I told him yes, he started cooking breakfast and we talked while he cooked. When breakfast was done we talked a little more and I decided to leave after a while.

A whole week and three days went by and Tyrus and I hung together every single day, but who was counting. I was out of school for the summer and when he got off work at 5 p.m. he was at my house by 6:30 or I was at his. He would go home and shower, change clothes and come right over or I would be at his house while he showered and changed clothes. Most nights I cooked dinner and he cooked a few times. We had so much fun around each other.

Tyrus took a trip with his home girl to Florida for a couple of days and he asked me if I would take care of his dogs while he was gone. He has a female pit-bull named Jada and a Chihuahua named Jacket, they were the sweetest dogs. He gave me a key and I took care of the dogs for two days until he returned.

After all this time I still didn't know if Tyrus messed around with men or not. I didn't even know if he was straight. He was good at hiding what he wanted to hide. The conversation of women or men never came up within our time it was when his friends came over to play spades at his house on Sunday night when I began to have my suspicions. I cooked dinner; cabbage, baked barbeque chicken breast, cornbread and yams. I was trying to impress him with my cooking. After the food was ready I headed over to Tyrus' crib.

His friends were all males and all gay. He looked straight and they never addressed him as "Girl, Chile, Hunny or Bitch." Most of us gay men use those phrases to each other. I continued to lead on as if I were straight too. I wasn't blowing my cover if he wasn't gay and generally 99 percent of the time my "Gaydar" is on point. We played a few hands of spades and people began to head out. I stayed behind and once everyone was gone Tyrus said, "Is dinner done" I laughed and replied, "Yessir!"

We headed over to my house, and then I fixed both our plates and had to reheat them in the microwave because the food was cold. Tyrus brought a blunt; we smoked in the process and flipped through the channels on the TV. Tyrus found something on HBO; we dimmed the lights, put the blunt out and began to eat. After we were done we were too stuffed to finish the blunt, we both had "Itis." My couch is a soft leather recliner and Tyrus reclined right on back and stretched out. Before long we both fell asleep. I woke up and it was around 4 a.m. Tyrus had on shorts and a wife beater and I had on the same.

While he laid reclined back I was laid out on the couch along with him. My head was right next to his thigh, well on his thigh in an "L" shape position. I honestly don't know how that happened because we both started out the same which was reclined back. My heart was racing, I didn't know if this was a sign to try him. I saw his entire body from head to toe. I could see every muscle, every curve. It was like he was glistening. Right when I was trying to decide what my next move should be Tyrus moved his leg over which caused me to put my head more on top of his thigh. My face was now directly at the head of his penis.

I knew then Tyrus was not really sleeping and was waiting on me to make my move. I was nervous but I slowly did it. I was looking at his dick intensely and once I saw it jump, I couldn't help but touch it, grab it and rub it. His dick started to jump and throb as he slowly began spreading his legs wider. After a few minutes passed Tyrus was fully erect and his dick was moving up and down. I grabbed and stroked his dick as I stood up and pulled down his shorts, helped him out of his beater and the rest is saved for my private memory.

For two months Tyrus and I had become inseparable. I knew some of his friends and his best friend Brandon became my close buddy as well. Tyrus was a very private person but he told his best friend everything. Brandon and I built a bond through Tyrus and he was rooting for us. I found out so much about Tyrus, he found out so much about me. I even found out his ex-boyfriend was one of my old flings.

I had gone to school with Tyrus' ex, he and I had a class together. He also played the straight role and out of nowhere he started asking me questions about oral sex. Long story short we had sex, he said he was straight, but he was dating Tyrus at the time. I would have never told Tyrus if he hadn't asked me did I know his ex because we went to the same school. He felt some type of way at first but got over it fast.

Tyrus made it very clear he wasn't looking for a boyfriend he just wanted to have his cake and eat it to. This was the same time he revealed he had a girlfriend. This bastard was living a double life and said his girlfriend knew of his "struggles!" He said he'd struggled with homosexuality for some time now and that's not how he wanted to live his life. Tyrus even said his parents approved of him but they believed he was going through a phase. His family was very church going so he was trying to live up to his parents image of a "Straight Man." I didn't understand why he was trying so hard when his older brother is gay too. **Blank Stare**

Tyrus wasn't going through a phase, Tyrus ass is gay! One night I was calling myself backing down from hanging around him, I met some guys online on Jack'd the gay website, they lived up the street from me and were roommates. I was in the process of writing "this book" it was late and I was bored. I wasn't looking for sex I just wanted to hang out and chill. I had only been around Tyrus for the last couple of months other than when Timothy came in town or Miyasha coming over.

I was chatting with these two guys on the Jack'd app when Tyrus texted and asked was I awake and if so what I was doing. I texted back and told him I was up writing in my book and we should smoke. It was around 4am, Tyrus texted back and said he had to be at work in a few hours, he would link up with me later once he got off work. A few minutes later I heard Tyrus car pull off out of the parking lot. He had dual pipes on his car making it very loud and I knew every time he came left.

I continued my conversation with the roommates Ben and Larry, they were attractive but we were not meeting on that note. I got their phone numbers and address and called them. We chopped it up for a minute before I decided to head out; they literally lived not even 5 minutes away. When I pulled up I called Ben to come out to meet me, it was still dark outside. Being I am still dealing with the near carjacking and beating in Dallas, Texas mentally I didn't like unfamiliar dark places at night and being alone. When Ben started walking out he told me he was coming up my way but to go the left and park.

I turned and looked to my left I couldn't believe my eyes there right behind me was Tyrus' car parked. When Ben got to my car before I got out I rolled my window down and asked him did he know the person driving the Camaro? Ben told me it was his homie "Tye" and showed me a picture of Tyrus. Tyrus called himself "Tye" his alias. My heart was beating fast and my mind was racing.

This bitch just hit me up and lied, said he couldn't smoke he had to be at work but he actually came over here. Not only did Ben show me the picture it was the same picture I took of Tyrus a couple of days prior in my living room. I asked Ben what they were doing in there. Ben said Tye came over to smoke and suck him and his homie's dick. I was blown away and pissed at the same damn time.

My dumb ass began having feelings for Tyrus. I knew Tyrus liked me but he didn't want to be with me. I didn't want to be with him either, I was cool with him having his girl and me at the same time but I wasn't looking for a relationship so having him on a regular was what I wanted. I didn't want him to be with anyone else other than the two of us. But Tyrus had something else in mind. He was a whore and he was not going to change for me or for his girlfriend, he cared nothing about, she was just his cover so people wouldn't know he was really gay.

When I decided I was going to leave and pull off Tyrus started walking out of the building. He saw Ben talking to me at my car and quickly walked a little out of the way to get to his car so I wouldn't see him but I saw him and I called out, "Hey Tyrus!"

He acted like he couldn't see me or he didn't know who the hell I was and yelled back "Who is that?"

I said, "Trey, bastard!"

Tyrus said, "Oh, what's good bro? I'll hit yo line later!"

I said, "Aight," in a sarcastic tone.

Tyrus pulled off and I went in!

The next episode I had with Tyrus made me want to punch him in his throat. We were at his house some of his friends who were over playing spades, smoking, sipping and eating when I noticed a new face. This dude was tall, lanky, brown skin and kind of cute and kind of ugly he was in the middle. I could tell he and Tyrus were into each other or he was just into Tyrus. Every time Tyrus said something the boy had something to say back. It was a smart remark or agreeing with Tyrus on subjects that were irrelevant. I was thinking this little bitch was trying to come in and get some of Tyrus.

I wasn't having it, yes I know Tyrus wasn't my man but I didn't want to share him with no one except the person I was already sharing him with. I knew Tyrus' girlfriend couldn't give him what I could. I had no issues with competing against her, actually I wasn't competing because there was no competition he really didn't want to be with her anyway. After a while I knew I had Tyrus' heart but his attention was with his girlfriend and every dick he could suck.

Tyrus finally introduced his friend. He said, "Oh my fault Trey have you met Hunter?" I said, "Naw kind of sarcastically though." Hunter said something smart in return and immediately I put him in his place with a hard direct look like I did real-estate! Hunter said, "I was just playing I'm kind of silly sometimes." I replied, "Well I'm not!" He caught my drift and we really didn't socialize the rest of night. I couldn't deal with him and I wanted to stick a spoon down his throat to gag him. I was on my Oprah Winfrey trying to be politically correct but Wendy Williams was trying to appear. #Petty

After the Hunter episode Tyrus wanted me to go to the club with him, Brandon, and some of his other friends. I was down to go at first when Tyrus said Brandon and some friends were going out. He called me back to let me know Hunter was going. I started having second thoughts but I still continued to get dressed. When I was ready and walking next door to meet everyone at Tyrus' house, I noticed Tyrus' ex-boyfriends car in the parking lot. Immediately I turned around and went back into the house. I was not about to hang out with them knowing one of them between Hunter and the ex would do something to get under my skin. I still wasn't done fucking with Tyrus.

Just the little things let me know where Tyrus was mentally. We rode around during the day and spent nights at each other's houses, we sleep together sometimes just with boxers on. He would hold me through the night and would look at me in peculiar ways. We treated each other out to eat, we would watch movies all night and lay against each other. Tyrus had a membership at Planet Fitness and I would tag along. He would show me how to lift certain weights to build certain parts of my body, I loved watching him work out and seeing him flex his muscles.

The final straw was when Tyrus texted me on August 17, 2015 asking if I would come over and hang with Brandon, his girlfriend and himself. I read the text and I started to text back "WTF!" Instead I texted back my favorite meme "Ester Rolle" (Florida Evans) from "Good Times" with her smiling sitting in a car with a seat belt on. Tyrus asked, "what does that mean?" I told him "it meant hell naw, what the fuck, I look like hanging with a bitch whose man I was really liking, sucking his dick, he sucking my dick and us fucking that wouldn't be right, right?! I'm already fucking her man and now you want me to smile in this bitch face! FOH" (Fuck Outta Here)

Tyrus texted me back and said "Because of you I broke my rules and acted on my struggle, you cool as fuck and I thought we had something. You're just like the rest of these Atlanta niccas and if you can't come over and hang with my girl and me then we can't hang no more! I didn't even reply.

Tyrus was the shit and I wanted to be with him, I didn't want to be with him, I just wanted to be with him if you know what I mean. I enjoyed when we had sex or did anything sexually. He was sensual and loving, he caressed my body without trying to have my mind. It wasn't hard not loving him it was hard not wanting him. Eventually we started doing our own thing and I was back to dating. After all that time Tyrus finally realized he was wasting his life living a lie and trying to live for others. He eventually ended his relationship with his girlfriend and got into a relationship with a man. We are still cool to this day and speak to one another if we cross paths.

I learned we met because he had to see what it was like to live his life and be free from me. We thought alike on many things but he couldn't see things a certain way until someone else said it to him. I was there to help him live in his truth and not go through life hurting people because he's struggling with something no one would ever understand just how deep his struggle is trying to please other people.

CHAPTER 9

#26 & #14

Here I was back talking to the guy I wanted badly and the same guy whose heart I'd crushed. All I could do was thank my Heavenly Father, I prayed for this too long. I wanted someone who would love me the way I loved them. I wanted for everything I liked in a man, all the 3 Cs and I simply wanted a redbone. I was ready for love however we always want what's not good for us and what's good for us we don't want. #26 could not let go of the fact that I cheated and I was pissed he threw it in my face every chance he could. I didn't understand him, some days he wanted what I wanted and other days he had his doubts.

We were going back and forth visiting one another it all started in late December 2014 a couple of months before I was set to graduate. I had been reaching out to him for a minute before he finally decided to reply. I inboxed him my number since we both changed our phone numbers. He called me one night and we talked until the next morning we actually fell asleep on the phone. At that moment I felt every feeling I'd ever felt for him come rushing back. I wanted to rekindle what I'd messed up. #26 was a great man and

I destroyed what we had by cheating. I was a changed person and I wanted what he wanted when we were first together, which was a long lasting relationship.

We started off by talking about the past and how we both messed up. I took most of the blame being I was the one who caused the breakup. I accepted responsibility I know we couldn't move forward if I didn't, I loved him and didn't care about apologizing because I was wrong. I posted so many things on Facebook about #26. I apologized so many times in hopes he would see them. I loved him and I wanted the world to know.

Number 26 was always spontaneous; he was in Atlanta the next day after my Miami trip. He called and said, "Samuel I have a room at the Hilton by the Airport come by when you're free." He stayed for a day that was the best birthday I had by far. He brought gifts, roses, shoes, fitted hats, cards and money, he was so romantic. The entire room was filled with nothing but colorful rose petals; red, purple, orange, yellow, pink and white. The roses had to cost him over $300.00. I'm quite sure #26 spent at least a rack ($1,000.00) on me for my birthday. He did all of this to my surprise and my bestie Timothy knew and he didn't tell me. This was the first time that bitch could ever keep a secret from me. I was glad he did because I truly was flabbergasted.

Before the month of May 2015 came and I was set to graduate I asked #26 if he would attend my graduation and book release party, we had been talking at that point for almost 5 months. He declined and said he wasn't ready to be around my friends and family he didn't want people looking at him saying he was a fool! I was heartbroken I knew none of my people would say negative things about #26 especially around him but I understood. I cared but I didn't care I was still doing the "dating thing" here in ATL and #26 didn't stay here. One monkey didn't stop no show but he did have my heart. I never loved anyone the way I loved him and Price.

Number 14 was honestly a rebound now that I think of it. He had problems and I didn't want to accept it. I had to be honest with myself after a while and realized #14 reminded me of #26 and that's one reason why I stayed with him for so long. The other reason was I felt I could change him. I learned throughout life you can't change anyone you have to accept them where they are. No one can change unless they want to change for themselves.

Several months passed and #26 and I were speaking about every other day. We would call each other in the morning to wake each other up, we would call at night and talk until one of us fell asleep. We would Facetime and have phone sex quite often. I was mentally with #26. Unfortunately I was still cheating I was seeing other people; the only difference was this time he knew because I told him. I didn't want to go into anything if there was going to be any lying, he understood and always told me to be careful. #26 was still HIV negative.

I loved this man #26 and we would send all kinds of pictures to each other. We laughed and joked on the phone at times it felt like he was in my presence. When we did have phone sex it felt like it went on for hours with us both Cumming multiple times. I liked our phone hook ups. **Don't Judge Me**

By the time August came you would have thought we were in a relationship. #26 took some vacation time and planned to stay in Atlanta with me for one of his layovers. My home girl Kim from Roosevelt High School came into town with her home girl Tyshell who also went to school with us they were underclassmen. Kim was my girl we both modeled together on "Esprit Modeling Troupe" in high school and our birthdays were a day apart with hers being on December 16.

I talked to Kim early in the morning of August 14th and decided we would hang out until Tyshell was out of her meeting. I gave Kim the address to my place and she came over about an hour later. Before she arrived at my house #26 called and said he was at the airport and here for his layover. He wasn't staying he had another flight to catch within the next two hours. When Kim walked in we walked right back out to make it to the airport before #26's flight left.

I was nervous pulling up the International part of the airport. #26 was on his way to Canada with his friends. I called him to let him know I was pulling up at the "arrival gates." He was at a different arrival door but was walking fast toward my car I was already standing outside of my car waiting for him. I wanted to see him walk up, I was anxious and I couldn't stop smiling.

Number 26 approached and I believe all the teeth in both our mouths were showing. He got closer I thought he was about to run towards me he was walking faster and faster. When he got to me he picked me up, hugged me tight and kissed me. I was elated, it was like a dream come true we both said we loved each other before we kissed again.

Kim said, "Cugh Cugh" as if she were couching. Hell, I had forgot that chile was with me. I was in a world with just #26 and me all alone. I quickly apologized to Kim and introduced them to one another. Kim said, "So this is the famous #26, I've heard so much about you and I know #26 isn't your real name!" #26 smiled and laughed and said, "No my real name is J---" she said that's what's up, nice to finally meet you J---.

I asked Kim to take some pictures of us it was like a photo shoot when we took pictures. We were hugging, smiling and kissing throughout the photo shoot and just like that, he had to go to make sure he caught his flight. He had to be back at the gate a little early because it was an international flight I was happy I got the chance to see him. I watched him walk away and once he was gone Kim and I left.

Kim and I went out to eat to Pappadeaux afterward. We hung out a few more hours and took some pictures before she had to leave too. She had to drive forty minutes to pick up Tyshell and beat Atlanta night traffic from where I lived. I was truly going to miss Kim I hadn't seen her since I was twenty-three or twenty-four years old.

Sunday afternoon #26 called to inform me he would be back in Atlanta later around 10 p.m. He wanted to see if I was going to be free and if so to come get him from the airport. Of course I was free, I didn't make any plans, I knew once he returned we were going to be spending the night together. When #26 arrived back in Atlanta he called to let me know.

I was already in route I told him to wait for me outside. I pulled up not even 10 minutes after his call. Once again we embraced as if we hadn't seen each other in some time. Soon as #26 got in the car he wanted to grab a bite to eat. I told him it was late and there were limited options unless he wanted to go downtown Atlanta. He decided to go to my place and grab something to eat nearby being I lived a good minute from the city.

We had a choice between McDonald's which I didn't eat, Burger King and Checkers. #26 chose Checkers I promised it felt like we were still together and had a break. When we pulled up he asked,

"Bae, what you want to eat?" I was shocked and ordered a Champ Cheese Burger and he ordered two Champ Burgers, a large fry, a six-piece mozzarella cheese stick, and an apple pie like he hadn't eaten since he left Canada.

When we arrived back at my house he sat down looked around and made himself at home. We both ate and watched TV and talked about his trip. After he was finished eating he wanted to take a shower he said he'd been in the air all day and felt sweaty and nasty.

I went and got him a towel from the closet and by the time I returned he was naked waiting to go into the bathroom. I passed him his towel then he asked where was mine; I smiled slightly and said holdup. I went back and got my towel while he started the shower for us. Once in the shower he began washing and kissing my body. All I could do was think of how I had torn us apart. We would have been together for 4 years if I did not cheat.

After he was done washing me he washed himself and I washed his back. When we began rinsing the soap off of our bodies he turned me toward the back of the shower. #26 grabbed a condom he had sitting on the edge of the tub and slipped it on. Before I knew it he was inside of me it was the best feeling in the world. I missed him and missed everything he had to offer me. I got my grove back just like that because nobody was hitting it like him!

Once we both climaxed we rinsed off again the water was running the entire time. He carried me out the shower to the living room all the lights were on and we were having sex on the couch. We were moaning, kissing and he moaned out the words I wanted to hear "I love you so much dude."

I said it back multiple times. We both climaxed about four or five more times and passed out on the living room floor.

We woke up the next morning around 8ish his flight left at 10:30 a.m. and he had to be at the airport within 30 minutes. We made it to the airport a couple of minutes before 9am. We both exited the car and gave each other a long hard kiss, I didn't know if that would be the last time I would see him but I wanted to be back with him after that night. When he walked away tears fell from my eyes. I felt like he was leaving me forever and I wanted him to stay.

I got back into my car after he went through the doors and I couldn't see him anymore and drove away. I had tears in my eyes, all I could think of were the "what if's." I wasn't even 10 minutes up the highway when #26 called and said he just made it in time, he loved me and he would call me once he made it back to NYC. I hung up the phone happy as ever. I had my man back in my mind!

Man oh man was this really happening with #14? Not even a week passed since #26 left and #14 was calling. It had been a good minute since I last spoke to him. After we broke up we remained cool but we talked less and less until I didn't hear from him again. Out of the clear blue sky #14 called my phone. He said he had gotten my number from Timothy. Usually I would be pissed if anyone gave my number out. I didn't care who the person was asking for my number I always told everyone "Don't give my number to anyone; I don't give a fuck who it is!" Here it was my best friend gave my number out, I was actually happy he did. I had no problems speaking with #14 and honestly I was kind of happy he did call. I couldn't believe that 2 ex-boyfriends loved me more than the man I married.

On the phone with #14 all I could do was picture him. He was a sexy redbone weighing 180, solid cut, stood 6 feet tall and was very masculine. #26 wasn't as masculine as #14 but he was a man.

They both were fine as ever to me and now I was thinking I wanted both of them. Speaking with #14 my feelings began to return, they were not as strong as they were for #26. My relationship with both of them lasted a year but I knew #26 longer.

Unfortunately I hurt #26 and I broke up with #14. #14 was an alcoholic and I couldn't deal he was drunk for breakfast, lunch, dinner and snack time too. He was drunk while he worked, drove around, had sex and basically just drunk 24-got-damn-7! I honestly don't EVER remember seeing #14 sober he needed alcohol for everything he did. Well #14 sure did surprise me with the information he threw upon me.

He called because he said he missed me and thought about his mistakes within our relationship and needed to apologize. He said, "I'm in rehab and I'm on Step 9. Step 9 is apologizing to those I've hurt." I was completely floored, I was happy he was getting himself clean. I always told him if he were clean he would be the perfect mate if not for me then for someone else.

Number 14 stated a couple of months after we broke up he entered into a new relationship. The man he was with was moving to San Diego, California and he knew of a great rehab for alcoholics. The guy wanted #14 to move with him and get clean. #14 stated the guy had been in love with him for some time. After he thought about it, he left his brother responsible for his lawn care company here in Atlanta, and moved to Cali with his "new boo."

I knew better, before we broke up I caught him cheating with another gay man. Throughout our entire relationship the only gay men he knew were my friends. When I saw him with his "new gay friend" I knew something was up. I didn't care long as he was taking care of home I was good. I wasn't about to waste my energy on that and he never threw it in my face.

Soon as they arrived in Cali the next week he went straight to rehab. He was almost done with the program when he decided to reach out to me while on Step 9. (There are 12 steps to the Alcoholic Anonymous program.) While apologizing he started to pour his heart out to me. #14 began telling me how much he loved me and wanted to get back with me. I was listening in disbelief, how in the hell are you in a program and apologizing to me. You're on step 9 which is to "Make direct amends to such people wherever possible except when to do so would injure them or others."

I couldn't get past the fact he was apologizing to me but about to hurt the person he was with because of me, he was about to start a terrible cycle I wanted no part of. We were talking and he sent me a picture of him, this dude looked so damn good sober I actually saw his eyes and he smiled in the picture. I'd never seen #14 smile and show teeth. His teeth were beautiful but he never showed them because he was always too damn drunk.

After I complimented him #14 sent a naked picture and captioned it "You miss this D***" I agreed with him to myself because I really did, there was never a problem with him in the sex department. I was confused and thrown off guard, how was it possible to be talking to both of my ex's at the same time, furthermore they were both on opposite ends of the United States. #26 in New York and #14 in Cali and here I was in ATL.

Before we hung up #14 said he was upset I missed his birthday and didn't call him. August 14 is #14's birthday and I missed it. #26 was in town and I was giving him all of my undivided attention. I didn't forget #14's birthday, I just didn't want to take my focus off of #26.

January 2015 after leaving TaQuan's birthday party in New Jersey Timothy, Dominique and I stopped to see #26, he was in Baltimore staying with family. He had a hotel room in downtown Baltimore for the weekend. He knew I was coming into town and the initial plan was to stay a day with him but that didn't happen.

I decided I would stay a couple of hours to make it up to him. Timothy and Dominique went and got something to eat and I stayed with #26. Every time I was with him it felt good I thought I was in heaven. Just his touch and the way he looked kept me wanting more. I felt my feelings growing deeper for him but I stayed grounded I knew he was never moving back to Atlanta.

Our past was messed up, I knew he couldn't get over it but in the hotel room for that time I learned to live in the moment. I lay in his arms and imagined how our future could have been. I knew he still loved me because he told me over and over during every stroke and kiss. Timothy and Dominique came back to the hotel and we got right back on the road.

I found myself speaking to both #26 and #14. Sometimes I would talk to them back to back, I would hang up from one to speak to the other. I couldn't believe I was having phone sex with them but at different times. They had no clue I was talking to the other in the manner I was but they did know I was socializing with them both. I still loved them but I really turned into Price acting like that.

CHAPTER 10

ROAD WARRIORS

The bestie and I've been hitting the road like crazy lately this was our second trip going to New Jersey. We went earlier in January for TaQuan's birthday party, this time we took Timothy's car. I drove the four hours to South Carolina to Timothy's house Thursday afternoon. I reached Timothy's place when he got off work. I unloaded my baggage from my car into "Cookie Lyon" Timothy's car.

It was natural for us to be in full concert mode the entire trip. By now we realized Beyoncé's "Scared of lonely" was our favorite song, every time we got in either car we sang that damn song. We switched up driving doing five to six hours apiece. When we were in Philly on the Girard Point Bridge a double-decker bridge I had to pee very badly. I screamed because of the fast moving traffic, people were going 90 mph and I was in the fast lane doing about 70 mph. I felt like the car was going to go off the bridge at any moment. There was water all around us and cars above us going in the opposite direction.

I hollered when a semi-truck flew past me doing about 120 mph and scared the shit out of Timothy he was dead sleep with his mouth wide open drooling. Timothy jumped up and said, "Bitch, what's wrong?"

I screamed out, "I gotta pee. I'm bout to pee on my damn self!"

Timothy said, "Bitch, you bet not pee in my damn car!"

We were still on the bridge I couldn't stop. Timothy told me to speed up so that we can hurry and exit off the first exit from the bridge. We got off on the first exit after the bridge and pulled over in front of someone house so I could relieve myself. We took Interstate 95N to avoid the toll roads and arrived in New Jersey exactly at 8 a.m. Friday.

We went straight to TaQuan and David's new place, they'd moved out of the condo into a new house. Their home was magnificent reminding me of a mini mansion made of brick with white trimmings that's located in a historic district of Newark. Their home has four levels, three stairwells, about 20 doors, over 50 windows, two ways to enter the main kitchen with two full kitchens, a bathroom on every level with three full and two half bathrooms making a total of five, and a roof deck.

After the coffee and 5-Hour Energy drinks we had to crash. I was jittery and felt like a zombie. TaQuan showed us around the house and where things were because they just moved in. He showed us our rooms and I immediately got in the bed. TaQuan had to go to work and that was fine with me, David was already at work before we arrived. I wanted to sleep but Timothy woke me up around noon. TaQuan took a half day at work and was due back at the house by 1 p.m. We showered and got dressed for the day then TaQuan took us to a Portuguese restaurant.

We drove to New York to visit Timothy's family. Soon as we got on the George Washington Bridge I felt a sense of saddness for the terror attack victims of September 11. I could see the new World Trade center from the bridge along with New York's skyline the view was emotionally breath taking. We rode around in Queens New York before picking up Timothy's cousin she was about to go shopping and of course we wanted to shop too.

We went to the Coliseum Mall located in Queens which took up about four or five city blocks we went into almost every store, I only bought shoes because I'm a shoe whore. We went into a tattoo parlor where we saw a fine ass red bone brother getting a tattoo and a couple of girls were leaving from getting their nose pierced. I wanted to get closer to the man so he could see me and the only way was to have something done so I got my nose pierced. The pain hurt like hell but it was well worth it the man and I were talking to each other while the lady was preparing my piercing and he was getting his chest tattooed. **My Slick Ass**

I was starving so we grabbed some hot dogs from a hot dog stand located in front of the mall. We visited Timothy's uncle who lived in Queens and dropped his cousin back off at her place before riding around downtown Manhattan and heading back to New Jersey. Before making it back to TaQuan's we stopped at a mom and pop shop and grabbed some pizza.

David planned for us to go to Manhattan to have dinner at BBQ's. We got changed as soon as we walked through the door. David, TaQuan, Nikki, David's best friend, Timothy and I headed right back out. BBQ's was thick and full of gays I mean it seemed like most of the gay men from NYC were in there.

Leaving BBQ's we headed to a gay club up the street well more like 6 downtown New York City blocks. The walk felt long and even longer by the time we left BBQ's we were all drunk. The line for the club was wrapped around the corner; TaQuan asked if we still wanted to go with it being filled to capacity. TaQuan told us New Yorkers don't play when it comes to clubs being over the capacity so we decided to leave. We were drunk as hell on the way back and David almost killed us driving 90 miles per hour on the toll road. David almost hit a car driving Timothy's car and all of us screamed.

David said, "I got this."

I said, "Like hell you do. Slow yo ass down!"

The next day was Saturday July 4th David and I went shopping at Willow Brook mall in Wayne Township I didn't have any shirts to wear and it was kind of nippy outside. I only brought wife beaters and 1 polo shirt because the weather app said it was going to be in the 90s all week. I guess I didn't look at the evening temperatures because it wasn't hot at all. TaQuan planned a barbeque later with their friends and family, he and I went to the liquor store to get the alcohol.

I thought TaQuan was going to buy out the entire store we walked out with six boxes of assorted alcohol from Tequila, Hennessey, Ciroc, Grey Goose, and some other shit and three boxes of Corona's.

I asked, "You think you have enough?"

TaQuan said, "We need alcohol for the house too!"

TaQuan started Bar-B-Queuing when we got back. I was loving my time at their place!

I had to change clothes again because I wanted to be grand, Timothy was already dressed and downstairs with David and Nikki some of TaQuan's friends and family started to arrive shortly after. Someone put the music on and then the spades table was set out. We all started introducing ourselves to each other before TaQuan came from outside and finished introducing everyone. It felt good to be surrounded by nothing but positive people.

We played cards, ate, sang songs, drank alcohol, took pictures, danced, talked and laughed the night away. It was an amazing atmosphere and I didn't even know most of these people. It's crazy how total strangers can accept you with no problems when your own family casts you aside. Everyone left close to midnight.

Sunday afternoon after getting dressed we rode the train to NYC, TaQuan paid for our train ride. When I say we walked everywhere I mean we walked throughout downtown Manhattan! I saw many things I hadn't seen since being in New York with James and Erin back in August of 2001. I saw the One World Trade Center, The Twin Towers Museum, where they filmed Law and Order and much more and even walked through Chinatown and shopped too.

I bought a Louie bag from a peddler on the street. Lots of people were out there trying to make money. Chinese people and Jamaicans were trying to sell me the same bag, some watches and cologne. All I wanted was the Louie bag! The Chinese woman told me the price was $120 at first, I told her I didn't have the cash and needed to go to the ATM. She directed me to an ATM across the street at a Bank of America. This lady followed me to the bank to get the cash, all the way there she kept asking me was I going to buy the bag for sure, I could pick a different one if I wanted to and she could give me a deal if I bought two.

By the time I got the cash and we all walked back I was approached by a Jamaican man. He saw I was talking to her about the bag and offered me the bag for $100 right in front of her face. The Chinese lady then countered at $80 the Jamaican man said $40 and I said, "You got yourself a deal, bro!" I walked away with the bag for only $40, but I think they were in cahoots. Either way, it's the same bag I seen in the Louie store online for $790!

I didn't care if it was a knock-off or not, it was only $40 and I was happy with that. Timothy got him a selfie stick I was glad he did he was getting on my got damn nerves about that fucking selfie stick. The ride back on the train Timothy and I sat on the subway benches and they were just cleaned with some bleach I was pissed I just bought my outfit the day before and now it was ruined a waste of $75!

After returning from NYC I decided to keep my outfit on, the bleach stain was kind of hot it wasn't a waste after all. We decided on grabbing some seafood, TaQuan took us to a grocery store where they steamed all the seafood. We ordered crabs, shrimps and lobsters there was so much food and it tasted great. I never had blue crabs before I stuck with what I know, the regular crab legs. We ate, sat back and talked the night away. We were leaving at 5 a.m.

Timothy got up first like always and got ready then rushed me to get ready so we would be on the rode by 5 a.m. David and TaQuan walked us downstairs we hugged and said our goodbyes before heading out the door we were on the highway exactly at 5 a.m. We pulled up to Timothy's in South Carolina precisely at 5 p.m. We got back faster even though we made a lot of stops. I drove back the 4 hours to Atlanta and arrived right at 9 p.m.

* * * * *

Timothy and I hit the road to Minnesota for my family reunion and for Timothy's birthday. My girl Michelle got us a free room at Mystic Lake Casino and Hotel. Michelle and I went way back to 2005. She and I worked together at Associated Bank, and I was her

Manager. She hooked me up with free rooms at Mystic Lake Casino and Hotel every time I came to visit. My cousin Felicia always told me I could stay with her but I wanted the privacy.

We left Atlanta August 20th the ride to Minnesota was a total of 22 hours. Timothy had to drive an additional four hours from South Carolina to get to me. We stopped in Indianapolis to see Moon, Gynder and my cousin Antawyone. We left there and stopped in Gary at my dad's house and spoke with my stepmother, sister and dad.

My mom brought us Lincoln sandwiches and we hit the highway straight to Minnesota but not before posting a picture on Facebook of the Lincoln's sandwich and my status had the location of Indiana/Chicago border. I wanted to be petty and let people know that I was just in Gary. **Side Stare**

I spent the night at Felicia's the first night and Timothy stayed with his friend Ms. Dee. That morning we checked into the hotel suite. We had a long day ahead of us and not a lot of time. We had to make the best of this trip because we only come once a year and the driving distance took up an entire day. Our first stop was to visit my grandma, I love my grandma, I had to see her and she was the main reason I was visiting. My grandma had just celebrated her 79th birthday I wanted to spend as much time as possible with her. Other than my father's step mother my grandma was my only living grandparent.

We made it to my grandma's around two in the afternoon. Timothy dropped me off and went to meet his friend. I hugged my grandma hard when I saw her. My grandma and I sat and talked, we both cried and told each other we loved one another. I think deep down my grandma was hurt by the way my mom is and has treated me and my siblings.

My grandmother told me she was apologizing for my mother's behavior. I told her she didn't have to apologize because my mother is a grown woman who makes her own decisions. My grandma and I talked about everything, more importantly my grandma was happy with the things I was doing and she told me she supported me 100 percent. By 4 o'clock Timothy was back and my grandma walked me out outside. She hugged Timothy and I and I told her I would see her the next day at the reunion.

We left and headed to Timothy's old job at AT&T he visited his coworkers for a few minutes before we headed to Denny's to eat. My stomach was in my back I was starving, I was always starving. After eating we left and went over to my Uncle Leon and Aunt Tami's house. A lot of family members were over there from Nina and her kids, Kurtis, Kyarra, Troy, Hazel, Nikki and her wife Keysha, Antoinette, some of my family from Michigan and others from Gary. My family was so supportive of my mission and I really appreciated it. Growing up with no support, to now having some of their support touched my heart.

Timothy left after one of his friends picked him up to go to the bar; he was celebrating his birthday with his friends and left me "Cookie Lyon." We sat around and reminisced about the past, growing up in the projects, our loved ones who are no longer with us and everything else under the sun. Later I left to pick up Timothy, and I got lost in the process. I knew where the bar was I just had a hard time remembering where the fuck it was.

After driving around for 30 minutes I decided to call Timothy and tell him I was lost. My ass needed directions to a place I had been to many, many times before and I lived in the city for 11 years. Timothy told me to use the GPS on my phone. I told him I did after a while but due to construction it kept redirecting me and not to where I needed to go. I finally found it after 30 to 40 additional minutes.

By the time I reached Timothy he was sloppy drunk in the bar he was loud and obnoxious. I ordered some chicken to eat up the little alcohol I drank and told him we needed to leave; it was close to closing time anyway. On the drive back to the hotel which was 55 minutes away Timothy had to throw up. I went from the left lane to the far right shoulder within a matter of seconds. I pulled over, and Timothy jumped out the car and started throwing up on the side of 35W. I was filming him the entire time and I kept telling him, "Hurry yo ass up, Bitch!"

Saturday, the next day we woke up right at noon Timothy had a hangover so I was going to be driving. We started out by picking up my little/big cousin Kenny he is my deceased Uncle Kenny's son, younger than me but he's bigger than me. He rode with us over to Felicia's, which is his older sister, Uncle Kenny has 10 kids. My brother and some of my cousins were over at Felicia's, everyone was going to leave out together to head to the reunion at the park.

Everyone started out trailing each other but somehow due to traffic and road closures and construction we all became separated. Part of Highway 100 was closed due to construction and so was Interstate 94. Nina called and said she was on Highway 694 coming around the opposite way, (694 is a circle around the city) eventually we all made it to the park a few minutes after one another.

Just about everyone came out, the food was catered, there was a DJ, the kids were playing at the park and we took family pictures. Nina and I took a lot of pictures together everyone knows Nina is my favorite I would give my life for my little cousin. The bright sky turned dark and it began to rain. Most of us decided to go to Dave and Busters before calling it a night.

We woke up early Sunday morning to be on the highway by 10 a.m., I needed to be back in Atlanta by 11 a.m. for school. This was the second week school was in session and I didn't want to start out missing days. We visited my grandma then hit the road.

By four in the afternoon, we ran into Chicago traffic and I was pissed! This was going to push us back and possibly make me late for class. When we made it to Gary we exited the highway so I could see my dad before I left. Being we were short on time I saw both of my dads for about 30 minutes each. I planned on going to visit other people but my classmate Amarro saw me on the Jack'd app and posted on Facebook that he sees that I'm in Gary!

I was livid and decided to leave I'd rather be safe than sorry. I wasn't trying to get killed nor did I want to put Timothy in harm's way, in addition I was now running behind two hours. We got through the traffic in Crown Point, Indiana pretty quickly after passing an accident and before long we were back in Indianapolis. We had driven about 12 hours at that point and switched up driving about two times apiece.

In Kentucky, I almost had an accident because the road ended. I thought I was exiting off because road construction was ahead, I didn't like driving between the cement wall barriers. Timothy was going to take over when I exited. It was extremely dark outside and instead of exiting off the road I got off on a dead end and at the end was broken up concrete blocks.

I was scared and shaking and Timothy took over driving. Timothy drove about 2 hours and I took back over because Timothy was tired, he had been driving for over 6 hours straight. I started driving again and when we got into the mountains of Tennessee it happened again, I almost crashed. The fog was thick and coming down from the mountains I started getting dizzy.

I pulled over to let Timothy drive, he was pissed but didn't want me driving. He didn't want to pull over either because of the fog. We rode out all the way to my house, Timothy ended up driving a full 14 hours by himself I did however stay up with him so he wouldn't fall asleep behind the wheel. We made it to my house at 10 a.m. I had exactly one hour to get to class but I had too many coffees and Red Bulls and ended up lying across the bed, falling asleep, and missing school for the entire day.

CHAPTER 11

THE UNHEARD VOICES

Everyone has a story within them. Everyone carries a cross; some are just heavier than others. The stories I have heard from people who've reached out to me were crazy some of comments were even crazier I couldn't believe the things that I'd heard. After hearing many stories I decided to take them all down and compile them into "The Unheard Voices." You will read what people have gone through, the questions that were asked of me and my responses.

In this chapter I decided to write all the inbox questions and comments. I wanted to let to let people know how other people think and how people have said that I just need to get over what happened to me and move on. Unfortunately I'll never get over it. I can live with it now and move on with my life. I'd learned to help others so they don't have to go through what I did by educating them, while other people I just simply READ!

The following inbox questions and comments from people are not grammatically correct! I just cut and copied people's messages and did not correct them at all!

***I wanted to let you know how your book personally touched me and help me understand some things to. You are so brave to put your life out there like that. I read your 1st book and was blown away but I was not ready for what was in book 2. I commend you young man. My sister has HIV and I didn't know really anything about it until now. I think I kind of treated her wrong after she told me but I am getting better with time. Thank you. You have purpose.

Thank you so much for your support! The story that was written was half the story that I wanted to write. I had planned a Book 3 and I was going to disclose my HIV status in that book. Unfortunately, being that my family put my status on FB, I had no choice but to let the world know. I wasn't ready but I had to face whatever was about to come.

I'm glad I did now because it was a burden lifted from my shoulders. I would be lying if I said I didn't care what the world thinks, but as long as my family and friends were behind me, I was willing and ready to face what was to come. It doesn't bother me like that, but in the back of my mind, I can hear the negative things. I brush them off for the most part because no one that says those things really knows me! They know what I have, but they don't know SAM!

I lost many people. MANY! But I still go on because there are other Sam's out there in the world. I had to be strong for myself and those people also. Love your sister hard. She will already be hit with rejection, and the butt of jokes, but as long as she has her sibling love, nothing else will matter much.

***I read your book and it was great. I would be so sad if I didn't have a relationship with my parents. I make sure to be close with my children because I wouldn't want them to feel not loved. What's your relationship with parents like now? I ask because I had seen your video that you said you wished your mom would be there to celebrate with you your graduation. Sorry if I'm being intrusive.

Thank you for your support. You're not being intrusive at all. Today, as far as with my mother, my relationship is the same; there's not one. We haven't spoken to one another since June of last year. That relationship is beyond my control. I gave it to GOD! With my father's, yes fathers, it's good.

No actually, my relationships with my fathers are great. My dad's love me and we speak almost daily. I'm getting closer with my biological dad and it's something I've wanted for years. From that relationship, I have an extended family that is incredibly supportive.

I know GOD answers prayers because I prayed for this relationship. Just like he answered that prayer, I know he heard my prayers for my mom and me.

***Your book was so good. I couldn't put it down. I was in a relationship before like you with a Price. I was dumb and naïve. I stayed in it for over 7 years. I'm single now for 2 years and I don't think I would date again because of it. The letter that you wrote to Price in your book had me rolling. It was deep and to the point. Do you have a relationship with price and you said you still love him just not in that way. What does that mean? Thank you again for your story. PS I hate being single lol

Thank you so much for your support. I think most of us have been in a relationship with a "Price" before. If we hadn't, we wouldn't know what real love really was. Most of us had to go through a Price to find what's right and what's not.

Fortunately, we graced the relationship of a Price then rather than now! You will date again love. You have to want to date and open your heart. Now you realize and can spot when someone is not right because your eyes have been opened. No one wants to repeat a cycle of bad relationships. But this does happen if you don't realize when someone is not right. It only takes most of us once to bump our heads. However, some people keep bumping their heads like crash dummies and never get it!

You understand now, so love will be sure to find you and you won't have to look for it. Put it in the atmosphere and watch what happens. I don't have a relationship with Price. I would like to. I know it sounds crazy, but yes, I would like to because I don't have any ill will, nor do I hold a grudge against him.

I once loved him more than I loved myself. That's what I meant when I said I love him but not in that way. You can love an ex and not want to be them. I love him because he showed me what love wasn't! I love him, because I am able to still love even after he broke my heart.

I am stronger today than I have ever been and I don't think that would have happened without being heart broken. But single isn't bad. You have to learn to love yourself and know exactly what you want, and unpacking that hurt baggage before you enter into a new relationship.

This is why you've been single for two years. You're just making sure the next relationship is what you want and ensuring it will work. MUAH

***I loss respect fo u eva sence u post dat shit on fb bout my homie. Old fag ass lying on my niggas

It's cool bro. I lost respect for you after you hit my home girl up asking her why she's supporting a fag! If you would have said that a year ago, I would for sure have cursed you out. Today and going forward, I'm learning to take the high road and put my positive energy into something that will yield me a greater return because your aren't worth my precious time.

However, all the energy you spent writing me this message, let's try putting some of that into getting a GED and loving your own child who's gay! If anything, you should be coming to me for advice because your son is the same age that I was when I started being openly feminine. I would think that's more important than anything else in this world, other than being worried about something that has absolutely nothing to do with you.

Your child, "My God Son," is growing up just like me and you're worried about a subject that you are not part of. What's more important to you; your home boy or your child?" Instead of throwing shade, I'd rather just shed the light, bro. You can hit me up on a better note when you get your mind right. I'll be here to educate you. Much Love

I read this book and all I'm reading are lies that you talk about P. (Price-Sam corrected real name) He is not like that at all. He's never lifted a hand to me. I dated him and he was the exact opposite. I read both of ur books. Sad story but you didn't have to lie on him. I've known him for two years and he is a gentleman to me. Ijs

Thank you so much for your support! I'm honored that you've read both books. Sadly, the proof is in the pudding, love. I don't even have to speak about him hitting me because it's all in the police reports. If you'd like a copy, I'd be glad to mail, fax, email or snapshot a picture for you. This way you will have the correct information. I don't speak about Domestic Violence for nothing!

Now, as far as him not being that way towards you is none of my concern. I am writing about me and what I experienced with him. Whenever you're ready for that information, contact me just the way you did here. MUAH

***Your not telling on everyone from the hood. It's not in either of these books and I know you were with more dudes. I just feel like if you gone tell it tell it all. Sorry bout what you experienced but it just seems like your telling on people trying to be messy and that's petty.

Thank you for your support. You don't know whom I've dealt with in the hood. Anything you know is speculation because you haven't heard it from me, and your damn sure not going to hear it from them. I told on those who had sex with me starting at the age of 12 AS A CHILD ONLY! I did this because I was a child.

Now, anyone that I had encounters with as a teen and up are not mentioned in either book, if that's what you're referring to. That's not anyone's business, including yours. Being messy would be like me saying, "I had a sexual encounter with Mikey D from 22$^{nd!}$"... RIGHT??!! Naw, that's not messy, it's petty **Shrugs Shoulders**

***Hey boo I loved your books. The 2nd book you touched on a lot that I suffer with. When I read about your depression and suicide attempt, I thought bout my life. Some people really don't understand those issues and I'm glad you touched on them.

Thank you so much for your support love. Depression and Suicidal thoughts are things that a lot of people deal with daily. Without getting help with Depression, it can lead to suicide. A lot of people think that if someone succeeds at attempted suicide, then they took the easy way out. That thought is sooooo not true. Suicide is the hardest decision anyone will ever make! The thought of taking your life will make you go crazy.

I was at my weakest moment in life and tried to make a selfish decision. This, too, was not going to be put in my book because I didn't want anyone to know. However, I was dealing with a lot and I didn't seek help. I didn't want pity or anyone trying to talk me out of what I was going to do, so I did the best thing that I felt was right. I tried, ALMOST succeeded, but GOD had other plans.

My advice to you is to find a coping skill. We all have them when the tough gets going. My coping skill is singing and praying. I'll listen to a song and SANG my heart out. If I don't know it, I keep it on repeat until I learn it. Find a coping skill and talk to someone that will just be an ear. Best of luck love.

***I just want to stop by and say you are one brave person. I come to your website most days just to listen to your story while watching your video on there. You are an inspiration to me. I commend you because I would never share my story with other people. I would not be able to deal with knowing rather they would still accept me or not. Your book gave me a lot of hope. May peace be with you.

Thank you so much for your support. I am honored that I inspire you. Sharing my story was very hard. I too thought about the rejection after each of my books was released. Here's the 2 things I learned: "Those people that want to stay in your life will be there. Those who mind don't matter and those who matter don't mind." People are going to talk about you regardless. So I figure, if they talk about me, at least they will be learning something.

I also learned that what most of us go through in this world, someone else has experienced it, or something relatable to it. With that being said, I choose to use my life as a guide. Granted some people may not like how it's presented or what's within it, but it's the life I lived and hopefully someone could use my mistakes and not make the same within their life.

***This book is insane crazy. I m sorry you went thru that stuff. I'm currently dating Price as you call him too funny. I know there is always 2 sides to every story. Price said it didn't that way. And none of this would have ever happened if you didn't leave him Dallas. I do feel that you shouldn't have left being that you did marry him. You should have sruck it out but you left and took everything he worked hard for. I say that was your karma.

Chile ... First let me say thank you for your support. You are not the first to be dating Price and he's told the exact opposite of what happened to. But I'm not going to even go into all that bro. It's kind of sad that you think my karma should have been getting my ass kicked and almost killed for nothing. Seriously, I had finally walked away and was moving on. I'll admit, I was the dummy for trying to save something that was dead. I learned a lot from it and I'm thankful that it did happen.

However, I do feel what's crazy is that you know about me and I have not a clue who you are. You are about the 10th boyfriend that has read my book/books and reached out. I guess someone really hasn't moved on after 5 years and still haven't signed any divorce papers. It shows because you shouldn't know my name, and that I wrote anything or who my ex was. However, don't feel special boo, you're about to be an ex soon too! MUAH

***How could be played like that? Your so outspoken and speak on relationships all the time and you got played hard. I felt so bad for you reading those parts but your bravery helps so many others like me.

Thank you for your support. A lot of us are stronger because of being played by someone. You either become bitter or better, stronger or weaker and I choose Better and Stronger. I also choose to help others so they won't have to be played and have to choose bitter or better etc….

Some people are not able to stand up, pick up the pieces and move along with life. They stay down and can't get over it. I say to those people, don't ever feel weak from someone belittling you or making you feel inferior. There are 7,393,702,375 (an estimate) in this world and you should not have to endure that from one person!

***How is your relationship with your ex ex lucianno?

Some people come into your life as a season, reason, and a lifetime. Lucianno came into my life for a reason. He was my ex ex. I hated him in the beginning. However, once he became ill from AIDS, (which he gave my ex WASband) we became the best of friends….for a season.

I learned a lot about my Wasband from Lucianno and I believe that gave me some sort of relief as to why my ex did the things he did and closure knowing that I would never do the things that he liked. I believe Lucianno was brought into my life for that reason and because he taught me about AIDS/HIV through him and the things of what not to do to have full blown AIDS. I walked away with this information that would last me a lifetime.

I will always love him for the love that he had shown me and we were able to put aside of the fact that had us at each other's necks in the first place.

***I just don't understand why you put your life on the book like this. I read your books and they are good but I don't thnk the book is the right place for that. Don't you feel embarrassed by people knowing yo life? Then you degraded yourself for a man from reading this book. Ithat's sad then you put it out there but they are nice books.

Thank you for your support. My books represents my life but also represents other people's lives as well. Wherever you can catch someone's attention is where you need to put what you're trying to get across. You see, I learned that I can't pay my bills by worrying about what someone is going to think about me. I can't be happy if all I'm worried about is what someone is going to say or feel about me.

I don't care because what happened to me happens to others and continues to do so as I type. That's why I put my life on FB. Trust me, there are things that you don't know about me. And, If you don't understand my mission, then you won't understand my story.

***How did you get over ur relationship with Price? I was in an abusive relationship and I can't shake him. I can't move on either because I still love him. Your books gave me strength to finally leave but I still feel like his prisoner. Please give me any advice

Thank you for your support. You made the first big step which was leaving. It's never easy getting over someone especially when you loved them wholeheartedly. And it's not right to move on with someone else thinking you will get over the other person. Hurt people hurt people, and you will hurt the next person until you heal yourself. Take some time to heal and remember the reasons why you left in the first place. That will give you closure enough to move forward and let go. Remember, you can't hold onto a shadow!

***What made you go to school after all this? I would have just died maybe a long time ago after reading what you went through. I am so proud of you. Keep on writing and helping others.

Thank you for your support. I could have just laid there and died but I choose to live. I actually wanted to live. I knew there was meaning in my life and I wanted to achieve everything that I ever dreamed of that was within my reach. Listening to the voices of my mother and Price (my ex WASband) telling me I was dumb and stupid for years, and not finishing college when I first started made me want to go back and get everything that said I couldn't have. You feel like nothing when the ones you love belittle you and try to break your self-esteem down.

In the beginning, I was doing this to prove them wrong. However, after attending college for a minute, I learned I was doing this for myself. I was proving to myself that I could and would do anything I wanted. I have the power to the rest of my life, the best of my life and that's just what I'm doing. Living life like it's going making sure I have more than I ever had.

***Just curious how do you feel about the families of the people you put in the book? I agree with you after I read the books. I was in a beauty shop here in GI and they were talkn about yo book. Some people was mad and some people were happy you did. I was curious as hell when I saw the book and I was like I'm getting me a copy. I ain't mad at cha baby!

Thank you for your support. I remember receiving many phone calls, friend request, inbox messages and more relating to my books at the Beauty Shop! I'm happy that it made people talk about what happened. I'm honestly happy I did put people's names in the book because it gave everyone a face to the names!

People need to know who molesters are. I can't sit and wonder what their family member's will think. From the last 4 years they've been pissed and that's fine. They will get over it. I've dealt with it for over 20 years and still do to this day.

I'm in a better place because of my actions and that's all that really matters to me. So if they don't like it, they can do what they've been saying they were going to do for the last four years ... SUE ME!

***It's sad that your out here dating and your still married. Do you even love your husband? That's kinda whorish in my opinion. I would never do that to my husband.

Thank you for your support ... But wait one minute. Did you even read the books thoroughly? Chile, my husband was cheating from the very beginning and I still remained faithful. My husband was cheating even after we were married, and again, I still remained faithful. Now after the Dallas, Texas situation and him wanting a threesome, I was done! How much more faithful can a person be?

I'm kind of lost as to how can you even ask me any questions about my marriage when you cheated on your husband and had a kid out of wedlock. But that's none of my business.

Yes, I do still love my husband, just not the way that you're supposed to love your mate. I love him for all the good things he showed me. And one more thing love, I'm not dating, I'm in a relationship!

***I read your book and understand your story. I feel that this is the reason that we can't stick together because of people bringing up stuff like this from the past. Please let it go. We can't have any unity because of this book. You are messing up peoples lives.

Thank you for your support. I'm not sorry that you feel that way. Most people that have not experienced what I have, and even some of those who have, always say, "Let it go, let the past be the past" and so many other things that they have no clue about "Getting over!" I wonder if your child, siblings or best friend had experienced what I have, would your opinion still be the same?!!

I'm not you! I am me! The same people that you're referring to that I messed up their life, ALMOST messed up mine. But basically you're saying that's okay, it's not a problem because it happened a long time ago and I should just move on! They didn't have a care in the world over what they did to me. If they did, they wouldn't have done it! So tell me, why should I care whose mad behind what I wrote?!

Again, I want you and my readers to know that was my childhood; something I can never get back. However, by writing my story, I can at least prevent another child from experiencing the same thing that I have or at least help them move forward if they do.

I'm not the reason there is not unity in our community! They are the reason. By them doing those sex acts to a child, they destroyed the Unity In Our Community! And shame on you for thinking otherwise! I understand you're upset, but Book 3 is coming soon so please get your cape ready because you're going to be Super Mad!

***Good Afternoon Mr. Holloway, I just had a personal type question. I'm going through a situation similar to yours in my life and it's been really tough on me. I don't know where to start... Well I found out almost a year ago that I have HIV and I contracted it from an abusive ex boyfriend that I knew was sleeping around on me. Not only did he admit that he was cheating on me, but I had mutual friends telling me that he was sleeping around and I caught him in the act. Anyhow, the relationship was on/off from 2010-2014 and has since ended. I have blocked him on all Social Media and deleted his phone numbers and haven't talked to him since the day we broke up. Ironically, he left me because of one indiscretion during the relationship as opposed to his many. All during the relationship I was the one supporting him, taking care of him, and helping him out when no one else would. I wasn't allowed to bring him into my home due to the type of person he was but I purchased him hotel rooms when he got kicked out of his residence, I would spend my entire paycheck to buy him clothes and anything else he needed/wanted and I even bought him a phone and he turned around and sold it for drug money. By now, you can probably tell how much I loved this guy. But I recently found myself being unhappy. Not only due to my "condition" (hate saying HIV) and because I feel as if I can't get over him. He was my 1st everything. First boyfriend, first crush, first sexual experience. I gave up everything to move in with him right after graduation and not only that my stupid self went back with him not once but at least 3 times after he had already caused me so much hell and pain. How did you manage to get over Price when he caused you everything you went through? And how do you remain so confident in your life and smile everyday? And I suppose my last question is, did you ever think that you wouldn't be happy and find love at first? And lastly, what made you not give up on love? – Thank you for your time and my apologies for the long message.

Thank you for reaching out, love, and I'm glad that you did. I went back to Price more than three times, so I have you beat!! LOL LOL LOL … I say that just to let you know you are not stupid for going back. You see, when we truly love someone, sometimes we tend to be naïve. We overlook many signs that a person outside of the bubble can spot quickly.

We sometimes wear blinders and block out the things that we don't want to see. Unfortunately, after a while, we have clear vision but it's often too late.

He was putting you down because he wasn't happy with himself. That's what a person generally does when they have problems. I managed to get over Price by consistently hearing him in the back of my head calling me dumb, stupid and saying no one would ever want me because I was weak minded. I know my worth, love, so I knew if I returned after the final straw I would be everything that he called me.

Chile, remaining confident is easy today. I was confident before I met him. Sometimes, we lose our self-esteem but once you look into a mirror and REALLY look at yourself, you will see you — a strong person that has made it this far and not given up because of a bump!

Pick yourself up, arrange your Tiara and keep it pushing. There is someone for everyone and love is right around the corner. I guarantee you, once you look at yourself in the mirror, you won't run into any person that's like your EX!

After my relationship, I had mixed emotions. I wanted love, but then I didn't. But I never gave up on love and GOD kept love within my heart. And today, six years after Price, I'm in love!

***I read this book and I was scared for you. Aren't you scared?

NO!!! I was scared for over 20 years stuck in stumbling place. I be damned if I live the rest of my life being scared! I've done nothing wrong!

***Hello Aurthor … we don't know each other personally but we are friends on Facebook … so and feel comfortable messaging u my thoughts and question … first off i want to say that I'm truly proud of u as a black man who have been though so much but still is so focus and determine to be successful … I haven't read ur books but from ur posts that u share with us on Facebook give me a good insight on past present and future … and because of what u share and still able to shine that beautiful smile make me even more proud of my black brother … now my question to u as black gay man….wait let me tell u a little story i had with a friend … we were talking about gay peole … mostly about how gay men looking and dressing like women and visa vese … my thing is i feel that who sleep with who u fall in love with is ur choice and business … but i don't like to c my black brother's dressing like and looking a woman … what's ur thoughts on that … thanks in advances … and i love u my brother…

Thank you so much love for support. I totally understand how you feel. As a child, being gay, a boy is dealing with his sexuality and the perception of the public. Some gay men are feminine and some are masculine. The feminine men choose to dress up because they feel like a woman. Not saying that they are, but that's their feelings. A masculine man is just like the Str8 men; they sometimes are hard to tell if they are gay or not.

Some gay men, like myself, have learned not to wear sexuality on their shoulders. Some gay men just don't care and choose to be free and dress how they feel. I was feminine at one time but I didn't feel comfortable dressing up like a woman. I like being a man, just not the manual labor stuff. They can keep that part! LOL LOL

I hope I answered that good. I would really have to talk with one of my gay friends that dress up or live as a transsexual to tell you more.

***WOW. That's all I can say. It hurt me to the core to read that your mother didn't love you the way a mother should love her child and she beat you on top of it. Witnessing your mother in domestic violence relationships how did you end up in one to.

Thank you for your support. I love my mother with all my heart. It's like this...I've seen this picture floating around on Facebook with a young boy. In one picture, it's a boy with a gun looking hard, and the other picture is a young boy that is gay. The caption on the picture reads...."What would you rather have, a young son who's a gang banger or a gay son?" I read so many replies that people would rather have the gang banger son because if they had the gay son, they would beat him straight! Welp, that's just what my mother tried to do. If that wasn't enough, she had me arrested; FOR BEING GAY! Regardless of all that, I still love my mother. Everyone can't be comfortable with having a gay child and loving them like you would if they were not.

When it comes to being in a domestic violent relationship, I learned what I saw. After every fight, they would love on each other and I constantly heard, "I'm sorry!" So when I was in my relationship, after the first fight that's just what I heard from Price, "I'm sorry and I love you!"

Yes, I never wanted to walk in my mother's shoes with being in a domestic violent relationship, but I didn't stop it when it first happened. I learned once someone puts their hands on you and you don't leave, it will happen again. I can't believe that I allowed myself to be in a violent relationship. But I Survived! I remember being thrown into a brick wall. But I Survived!

Now when you know better, you do better. I know better now.

***I will be suing the publishing company who published your book! You had no consent from my brother to put him in that garbage.

Please do! I am that company you will be suing! Not one of the men listed within both books gave me consent to list their names. I did it because it's the truth. Please go ahead and try suing me. I've been waiting for four years and it's long overdue. Guess I'll see you in court, but I won't hold my breath.

***I had to stop following your Eyes without a face page because I am already yo friend and see the same thing twice. Lol

Girl, bye! I don't follow every page that Beyoncé has but I follow a couple of them and I see the same thing many times. You are also following a couple of Beyoncé's pages and, well you get the point.

***Boy oh boy I just finished reading both books and I am amazed at you for continug to keep smiling. How in the hell do you do it? I am not strong like you at all

Thank you for your support. You are strong! Never think you're not! We become what we speak so you have to speak differently! People always ask how I continue to smile and be happy after all that's happened. I always stay optimistic. It's because I have confidence in myself that I can overcome anything.

***I read both books and I'm pissed my childs father is no way DL and Im going to write a book and tell the world your full of shit.

Well, WOW… Thank you for your support, love. If your child's father is in my books, it's not a lie! That's a sign for you to open your eyes if you are still with him. I didn't write these books and include real names for nothing. When you're done writing that book, go to Bowker.com and purchase an ISBN number and Barcode then go to gov.com and copyright it. That way you can be self-published. When you are writing about me, please mention my full name, "Samuel P. Holloway III" a couple of times. That way once you're finished, published and it's out for the public to read, I can show you what it means to sue someone for libel. This is what your child's father should have done to me! ☺

***I loved your books. I'm just not sure why you are putting men out their the way you do. I think that's real petty of you and I feel that you are just trying to hurt people because ur angry.

Thank you for your support, love. Let me be the first to tell you, I'm not angry, or being vindictive or trying to hurt anyone. I am looking out for my sista's whenever I post ANYTHING about DL MEN! I have sista's, nieces, female cousins and friends. How would you feel if you found out one of your peoples were dealing with a

Why Did We Meet? — It Wasn't' By Choice

This is my second cousin who molested me as a child.
Markell "Kelly" Edmonds — Child Molester

DL Brother and they had their heart crushed by him because he was seeing another man and/or had contracted AIDS/HIV from them?!

I believe you would feel how I would feel. So, I believe brother's should GSAC= Give Sista's A Choice…

Some of our sista's already have trust issues because no father was in their lives and or being raped/molested or dogged out. Then to top that off, some men do so much lying that it's hard for the sista's to trust the next man … and if that wasn't the tip of the iceberg, some brothers have that their "Interested in Women" (On FB) when they're really "Interested in Men!" What do you think about that?

***I haven't read your books because everybody saying you lying.

Hello, you should really read the books then. Not saying that it will make a difference in your opinion or the way you feel, but you should read before you comment. All that matters is I wrote them, told my story and still have not been sued yet! But I will say this, be careful when you blindly follow the masses. Sometimes the "M" is silent. ☺

***Your books helped me so much. After my cousin read them she gave them to me. Your story gave me courage to tell my mom and I was gay and her brother had been molesting with me since I was 6. She don't believe me and it hurts but I feel better that I told her and she knows I'm gay. Its hard out here and I went through a lot of bullying here. I am now home schooled because I hate going to school and I want to say thank you for talking to me and my mom.

I'm glad that I was able to help you. We all go through things in life and it's to make us smarter and stronger individuals. Don't ever allow anyone to bring you down and belittle you or make you feel afraid of them. You have the power!

Your mom will come around soon. That was a hard pill to swallow for her and you just have to give her time. It's never easy dealing with the outcome of telling a parent that their sibling molested their child. However, you're cousin felt that something was going on and that's why she reached out to me. She wanted you to come clean so you could be free and happy.

Go on had and smile now, lil brother. GOD never left you and always remember HE gives his hardest battles to his strongest soldiers. You are never alone and I am available when you need to talk. This is your senior year so go hard. You got this!

***Did you ever confront any of your molesters? And if you did, How did you feel after you got it of your chest. OK if you do this do you do it for closer or do you do it for peace

Yes. I have only had the chance to confront two of my molesters out of the nine. Seven of my molesters were my brother's friends. Well, *are* my brother's friends because he seems to still converse with these fools. SMDH!!!

Two of my molesters are my second cousins. I had the chance to confront Maurice "Munk" Moody over the phone while he was in prison. I explained how that conversation went on for a couple of months. He stated that he didn't think he did anything wrong because we were close in age and that he loved me. It went sour after I posted bits of our conversation to Facebook.

I also confronted one of my second cousins. I hit him up on Facebook. I was shocked when he asked who was I? So I replied back and said your cousin, the little boy you used to have sex (explicit word) with! Then I stated do you remember me now? And to my surprise, he answered back and just said, "YES!" I screen shot the conversation and ONLY sent it to my family!

I felt better after confronting them both, but that wasn't enough. I want my justice! I confronted them for peace. Peace in my heart. There will never be closure because I will never forget what they did. They took away my childhood and I can never get it back. But I have peace in my heart regardless.

That's why I do what I do, to ensure no one else has to find peace in their own hearts from something caused by someone. That's another reason why I'm trying to change the law of the Statue of Limitations. We need to do away with this law and have SAM's Law. This law will allow us to seek justice no matter how long we wait! Please sign the petition and tell your friends and family about it too!

***I read the book but I didn't really understand why you changed your name. I'm not judging but I would have kept the name my mom named me after all it was your dad name.

Thank you for your support. I changed my name because I wanted my birth father's name. I wanted to carry on his legacy. I honestly hated the name Robert. I love my dad, the man who raised me, but that name carried too many demons.

My mother's boyfriend whom molested me also name was Robert Jackson. I didn't want any affiliation with the name Robert. I wanted a change and this was my way out after establishing a relationship with my birth father. And I really love the name Samuel Percy Holloway III.

***Yo I thought this was goin to be a gay book. I was at a barbershop n the G n everbody was talkin bout this joint. Bro I have much respect for you. I don't know if I could have did that. If you were my brother or my child these fools a be dead. You gon help a lot of peeps yo

Thank you so much for your support, bro. It really means a lot. I wish more brothers think the way you think. So many of us are scared to support something when we should be looking at the message rather than the person. This is not a gay story and I'm glad you recognized that as a straight man! This is just a story that happens to be told by a gay man. At the end of the day, I'm still a man and this is not just my story.

Too bad you're not my brother. My brother still socializes with my molesters because they are "Friends!" Sometimes I think to myself that if I had a little brother or a child or even any of my family, and what happened to me happened to them, what I would have done. While trying to process that thought, I keep seeing myself sitting in someone's prison cell. But hey, different strokes for different folks. My whole mission is help others!

***Do you ever think about Price? I was used and abused and I can't move on. I keep going back and he keeps on using me. Is this a gay thing? I see you in new relationship and I want to be like you cause you look happy as fuck

Yes, I think about Price. Not as much as I used to years ago though. Eventually the love you had will start to die down. It may never fully go away, but the more you value and respect yourself, you will understand why you are free from that person. You can move on.

As long as you keep saying that you can't move on you won't! What you speak comes into existence so always be careful with your word choice. Sometimes, we have to keep going back to be hit so we understand fully that the situation is not for us. Unfortunately, some of us bump our heads too many times and after a while, we are stuck there.

This is not a gay thing. This happens to everyone regardless of sexual orientation. It's life. However, you don't have to deal with it forever. The choice is yours. You already made the first step of moving on by admitting that you know you are getting used.

And yes, I am in a relationship. It's not really new. I just didn't tell everyone when it happened. When you know your worth, you won't settle for anything less!

***I am so sorry I've been praying for god to forgive me. I ask you for you forgiveness. I'm crying saying why me why my child. I called you a liar and a fag please forgive me. My child was molested and I'm going crazy. This mother fucker messed with my baby. I called the police but my boy needs help. Please call me Robert I am so sorry. Please call me 219….

After speaking with this mother for a couple of days, my heart was broken. We have to stop being quick to judge someone because of their shell. Molestation happens to men and women and just because a person is gay does not mean that it didn't happen or the person wanted it.

As women, you all have to understand that just because you've slept with someone does not mean they won't sleep with a child; boy or girl. As men, you have to realize that your homie has a separate life that they won't speak about. These men will lie as if they were trying to stay out of out jail! Signs are everywhere these day and some people remain naïve, ignorant and turn a blind eye to a devastating situation. Please start paying attention!

*** Are you offended by the gay jokes?

I'm not offended by gay jokes, sometimes. It all depends on the joke and the manner in which it was delivered. Delivery is everything! Sometimes I crack gay jokes on myself. As long as someone is not trying to belittle or call me out using a gay joke, I'm cool with it.

***I think you should think before you post all this personal stuff. Once it's out their it can't be deleted.

I do think. That's why I ask people to share and tag others once I put it "out there!" I thought long and hard, that's why I have not one but two books out there full of personal stuff! Hopefully I can educate and help people. Furthermore, I can't stop thinking of all the personal things about me, so I'm putting out more in Book 3! Maybe, just maybe, I can save a life!

CHAPTER 12

COLLEGE LIFE

I absolutely love college life this is a place where I truly wanted to be. College felt different to me it was a second chance at a higher education. It reminded me of school on many levels but there was a huge difference, for the most part everyone was respectful. Going back to school after obtaining my Associates Degree made me feel I could accomplish anything I set my mind to.

This was a long time coming I was kicked out of school when I first moved to Minnesota in 1998 because of funds. I couldn't afford to pay for school I was an out of state resident and I didn't want a student loan. It took me 16 long years to go back to school but I was glad I made the decision to do so.

I loved one of my professors more than anything in this world. Professor Franda Clay is a GODsend, she is always there when I needed an ear or a hug. She hugged me every day we had class and anytime she saw me I love her so much. I always say we all have a story within us and some of our crosses are heavier than others but we all have a cross. Franda is my mentor; she is a strong woman who wore her tiara like a true Queen. She has 2 daughters, a single parent, a widow, and does side teaching jobs and shares a lot of knowledge and love.

Diane is another person from school I love. Diane is my sista in school I called her "My school sista." We both share a bond because of our past and our passion. Her ex-husband is very similar to my ex-husband we grew closer to one another especially when one of us was down. Our passion to help the youth is what forged our bond; we both feel no child should go without being loved.

Diane and I were together at school 24/7, we had every class together on our mission to complete college with both our Associate and Bachelor degrees. We helped each other with work to ensure we maintained a high grade point average. We celebrated each other's successes, we both made the Dean's list! She took part in my making videos daily to document the days in college. We took pictures all the time and interacted with our peers to participate, Diane is my sista indeed.

I've met many new people while in college, I learned college was about working with others, meeting deadlines, doing projects and assignments you really didn't want to do. College was simply a job and networking with others. It was fun going to school (work) and learning something new every day. However, on the other hand lecture classes, depending on the professor, were boring. Some professors loved to hear themselves talk they spoke during the entire class with a monotone voice. I hate online classes the work load is heavy and the time is not enough to put everything you have into the work. Professor Clay and a few other staff members were my favorite.

I've had great college classmates. I've taken my fair share of tests, exams, quizzes and pop quizzes. Within my years at Atlanta Metropolitan State College I only received 3 bad grades. Even though I failed those classes I took pride in making them up. It is true when some people say a professor doesn't like them I had a professor who I knew didn't like me he showed it every chance he got in front of whom ever and whenever.

He was disrespectful, he didn't care, I came in late to his class on a couple of occasions; he would never allow me to sign the attendance roll. One day I came in exactly 12 minutes late, per his syllabus if you are 15 minutes late you are considered absent. This professor was always late, our class initially was set to meet two days per week from 8 a.m. to 9:20 a.m. He changed it to only meet one day per week and from 8:30 a.m. to 9:20 a.m. because traffic was bad where he was coming from and not to mention some days he would cancel class and not notify anyone. So what's good for the goose is not good for the gander?! **Blank Stare**

On the day I came in late I sat down and was preparing to take notes. He was lecturing, he was always lecturing about "nothing!" He stopped and told me right in front of everyone "Mr. Holloway you are going to fail this class you are consistently late!" Before I knew it I had forgotten he was my professor.

I immediately told him "Excuse me Mr. (Professors name) you will NOT address me in that manner in front of this class! If you want to address me, you speak to me one on one, in your office or after class, don't ever disrespect me in that manner again." He got the message and shut the fuck up! How dare him call me out when this other girl comes in late every got damn day and sometimes 15 minutes before the class is over, but he will call her up to his desk to sign the roll, she wore sun dresses every day. **Get The Fuck Outta Here Bastard**

I wasn't having it at all and you only have one time to disrespect me! I went straight to the "Dean of Students" but not before

I contacted some lawyers. I was ready to sue on the bases of his threat that I was going to fail his class. He would score my papers the lowest out of the entire class for homework assignments. I had proof by getting everyone else's score and comparing them to mine. Needless to say, the situation was nipped in the bud after my meeting. You won't do me!

I also had a fine professor. Oh boy, was he fine! He taught Biology and Biology Lab. I failed both classes the previous semester but in his class I really paid attention, I had to! He was a red bone about 200 pounds solid, very masculine, deep voice and seemed to stare at me sometimes and he was very single. I would always ask questions and stay after class for things I didn't understand when he went over the lesson plan. I passed both classes with a strong B!

I only encountered two arguments while in school. I didn't allow them to escalate I was at a higher point in my life. There was one young lady and one guy that didn't like me. Some ladies always seemed to not like me for some strange reason. I am a real cool guy once people get to know me however they were often distracted by my shell instead of feeling my heart, usually because I am gay.

This girl got in my face in the computer lab after she sat at the computer I was using when I left to go print papers. My things were still there and she moved them to the side and started using the computer closing out the windows that were open. I asked her to move and told her I was using the computer and I went to print papers. She declined to move, I politely slid her things to the side and asked her to get up again.

She got loud and the security guard came over. I explained the situation and he made her get up. The security guard told her to leave because she was being belligerent calling me all types of things from "Fag, gay dude and sissy." Those were my trigger words but I didn't say anything I had work that needed to be turned in and I was a college student not a high school student. When I was done I left the lab building and she was waiting for me outside she was still angry and started calling me names.

Onsemious was walking up and caught wind of what was transpiring. She threatened to call her boyfriend to come up to the school "to beat my fagget ass!" Onsemious wasn't having it and told her "If yo boyfriend bring his punk ass up here talking shit to my boy we gonna jump his ass!" She thought twice, shut up and walked away. They were from the same hood. I reported her to the Dean of Students later after I turned my work in, I wasn't having the drama.

This guy in one of my classes would say smart things about me in class for example, "Ole boy ain't got no clothes, he only wears white tee shirts or hoodies and he is the teacher's pet." I was not the teacher's pet. I asked questions whenever I didn't fully comprehend something. I didn't really dress up during that time, it was hot outside and cold in the classrooms and I was not there in college to impress anyone I was just there to learn and get my degree.

Instead of snapping out, I clapped back and told him, "You doing all that talking but you have a bus card falling out of your pocket," then I dropped my car keys with the Kia fob. He didn't say anything after that and the people in the class were all like OOOHHHHH! **READ**

On our last day of class right after finals we had a potluck in class. All the students brought a dish, chips or drinks. Just about every professor I had allowed me to sell my books in class. I even had some professors who made my books extra credit if students purchased them, read them and turned in an essay about what they read. I would have to give the name of the students to the professors who actually purchased a book my professors where huge supporters by helping me make others aware. I had some professors help me with my 501 C3 for my Youth Organization.

The food on campus was good but it is expensive. A pasta bowl and drink was almost $10. A sub sandwich cost more than a Subway sandwich. But if you were hungry you ignored those prices and got your ass something to eat. The staff members with the exception of 1 were fabulous. They were all personal and made the students feel wanted; at least that's how I felt. The school held job fairs all the time to help students find good paying jobs.

During Finals in April the school held a "Spring Fest," it was to ease our brains during final exam week. They catered homemade ice cream, funnel cakes, snow cones, hamburgers and hotdogs. They had 3 different bouncing houses, raffles and gave away an assortment of prizes from T-shirts, hats and key chains. I always had fun on campus.

* * * * *

I wear many hats living here in Atlanta. I'm an Advocate who speaks at many different events and functions, I've helped people cope with their AIDS/HIV diagnosis when they found out their tests results, a full-time college student, an author and most importantly, I wear the hat of being a good friend.

For someone who had a serious issue trusting gay men, today I have a circle of male friends both straight and gay. The gay friends I have at this point in my life make my circle complete and I trust them all without hesitation. I love how they have my back when things arise, they don't play and neither do my straight male friends!

I am a mentor to many of my straight friends. Onsemious is my best straight friend. I would give my last to him if he needed it. Onsemious has been there without judgment and has even lost a girlfriend because he's my friend. One day while kicking it in the very beginning of our friendship his girlfriend came over. Onsemious and I were playing the card game "Trump" he told her about me before and that I was an author.

This chick goggled me and found out I am HIV positive and gay. Onsemious hadn't told her any of that! When she came through the door she had an attitude soon as she looked at me. I had never met this young lady in my life and at this point I'd only heard nice things about her.

I spoke and she gave me the meanest look and went straight to Onsemious' bedroom. Onsemious said, "don't mind her bro she tripping for nothing." Immediately she called Onsemious to the room, she yelled at him and asked why did he have a gay man in his house who has AIDS?!

Onsemious said, "Who the hell am I to judge that man, what he does and what he has?" She said, "I think he should leave right now!" I could hear her, she was very loud and his room was down the hall from the living room. They were behind a closed door but she obviously wanted me to hear everything she was saying!

Onsemious told her, "If you don't like him because of that then you should leave!" His girlfriend opened the door and said, "You want me to leave so you can hang with a fag that has AIDS?"

Onsemious told her, "That was not even necessary and dude cool if you got to know him but since you feel like that and you're being hell of disrespectful you can get the fuck out, NOW!"

She stormed out the room and down the hall to the living room. I was sitting there just looking at her. I believed my face showed I that was pissed but I took the higher road and simply said, "It was nice meeting you too!"

She said, "Fuck you!" as she went out the door.

Onsemious has never changed since day one and he will snap if anyone disrespects me. I will forever love him for being true, regardless of what I have and what I am.

Onsemious' mother loved me too. His mom would cook Sunday dinners and would tell Onsemious to invite all his friends. She couldn't cook for shit in the world but it was the thought that counted. His mother's greens would be either crunchy, because they weren't done or gritty because she didn't clean them thoroughly. Her barbeque would always be undercooked and I don't even want to talk about her potato salad.

Nonetheless I showed her how to cook greens and ever since her greens have been on point. I've been shopping with just her and I remember one time we were out and about and talking and she said, "If my son were gay I would love to have you as a son-in-law!" That made me smile hard as hell although Onsemious is straight and I didn't look at him in that way. His mom hates his new girlfriend. I think his girlfriend is cool but she can't cook either. I told Onsemious he finally found a girl that cooks just like his momma!

Cody is Onsemious' best friend although we've all known each other the same length of time we all went to school together and met each other in Math class. Cody is a basketball head but has a very short temper. Other than that he loves to spend his money when we go out. Cody is one of those friends that will give it if you need it I loved that about him. He would call some days and be like, "Bro, you good, you need anything? Just checking, man."

These two together is are whole mess they both keep me on my feet and a smile on my face my sexuality has nothing to do with our friendship. They both have gay cousins and tried to hook me up with them but both their cousins are dogs and have run through our gay community. Cody's cousin is very well known, he's a popular DJ here in Atlanta everyone also thinks his cousin is straight.

Dutch and Lenora were my next door neighbors at one point they were the cutest couple. Their daughter is absolutely gorgeous, every time she sees me she runs to me and hugs me, rubs my head and laughs, I think she thinks I'm a pet! She says, "Mommy there's daddy's friend," then reaches for my phone and holds it to her face. She loves taking pictures and every time I see her we take a couple of selfies. She is so grown she would want to see the pictures after I took them she would say, "That's cute!"

Carlos and Smooth were also my neighbors at one point, they're cousins and both straight, they're both fine as hell to me. I never crossed the lined with them I valued our friendship, but they're still fine. Carlos is 6'3" or 6'4", redbone, bowlegged, ripped, has a very deep voice and a thug. When my cousins came to town from Minnesota they thought he was GOD's gift to women! I told them to stay back because he will play they're ass like an instrument!

His cousin Smooth was 6'1" or 6'2", dark skin, about 180 pounds solid and also a thug. They both worked for the city but after five are street pharmacists, both from Atlanta and did I mention fine?! **Smiling Hard** Hanging with them was nothing but love. A man who is comfortable in their own skin and cares less of what anyone else thinks about them is the real definition of a man. A man who worries about what people think if he hangs around or knows gay men and calls gay men out are the men you have to look at sideways.

I remember us all riding out to Lenox for Mother's Day 2015. They were shopping for their mothers and girlfriends, their mothers were sisters and their mothers loved me. Carlos mom would throw cook outs and have her gay friends over I had the best of times hanging over her at house. They also have a gay uncle; their mother's brother is gay. I believe that is a main factor in why we were cool. All of these friendships were unexpected and I've learned those are the best ones to have.

* * * * *

After I obtain my bachelor's degree I want to enroll in law school. I want to become a lawyer in the next three years. I figure why not, I'm going to be 41 whether I go back to school or not. I'm going to represent the young girls who were molested and women who were raped by Stacey "Ray" Whitt for "FREE" they will have justice I'm speaking this into existence!

CHAPTER 13

DEUCES

I know Domestic Violence all too well. I legally married a man and within the relationship I lost my self, my values, morals and almost even my life. My ex beat me twice the second time more severe than the first. He threw me into a brick wall and left me dazed and dizzy and not even 2 months later he set me up. I was nearly killed by the men he was sleeping and cheating with.

When I awoke I didn't know who I was. My teeth were broken from my gums, ribs broke, and finger broke, and cuts and bruises everywhere. I was declared legally paralyzed on the right side of my body. After a total 7 surgeries I am still here! I am still alive! But GOD! But GOD! My GOD is a mighty GOD and love still wins!

I went through hurting for 8 months after our breakup I was truly broken I thought. I learned we were not made to break, bend maybe but never break! I had to learn to deal and cope with the devastation of being cheated on by my ex-husband with my friends, his friends and those he called his "cousins" it wasn't easy. I went through it all but I had to stand up again and be who I was before I met Price.

Why Did We Meet? — It Wasn't' By Choice

Price and I were separated longer than we were married how long was this going to take. I was tired of being tied down to someone who didn't want me. After all this time finally realized my worth I didn't want him. I think what was the worst part ever of being married to Price was this bastard gave me an ultimatum about signing the divorce papers. His sad ass wanted money that was nothing new or surprising.

I really hate I have HIV to this day I still can't believe I was so naïve, dumb, blind and ignorant to the fact. I allowed myself to be infected with HIV from being in love with someone I didn't even trust. My ex-husband was a complete whore, he fucked anything with a hole accept pussy and anything with a dick, he was a versatile nasty ass uninhibited freak. 2+2= my ex, that mother fucker was 4 everybody. Sad part was he also learned sometimes the grass is not greener on the other side because it's fake!

Now don't get me wrong, we are all freaks but when you're married every fantasy is not supposed to be a reality. My ex-husband had sex with anyone and didn't wear condoms after a certain period. I talked about the situation in *Eyes Without A Face* where I found a condom in his pants pocket and we were tested together at first and later on he found out he was HIV positive along with a few other STDs. Amazingly a few months later I only tested positive for HIV and not the other three diseases.

I decided to let my Townhouse go, it was the final straw of anything that would tie Price and I together. I already filed bankruptcy in 2009, after I got caught up in the mortgage scam with a couple of properties worth over a million dollars. Price wanted half of everything from the properties and fifty percent of the book sales. **Fuck Outta Here**

I rather let all that shit go back to the banks before I would put a damn penny in his pocket, as long as my credit was straight I was straight. I knew the mortgage business so getting a couple more properties was nothing. I needed this divorce for closure, more importantly I needed it because Price knew the "California Law." Per California Law whatever a spouse has it must be split between both parties 50/50 and they automatically have rights to everything after 10 years of being married rather you're separated or divorced. This year August 4, 2016 makes 8 years we have been married.

"Gay Marriage" didn't come easy and receiving a Gay divorce was going to be even harder. Gay divorce was new and came with many stipulations; I learned quickly I was going to have to fight the hardest legal battle of my life. My first attempt to seek a divorce was January 5, 2012. I filled out all the paper work and mailed the documents needed for the divorce, along with a check for $499, to the "San Francisco Courthouse" where we were married August 4, 2008. Not even a month passed before all my documents were sent back and the file was documented "REJECTED" in bold letters. I was crushed!

On my second attempt, I drove to Chicago it was my 15 year class reunion. I had been talking to Price since the month prior about the divorce. He assured me if I came to Chicago we would go to the "Daley Center" and file the divorce together.

My "little friend" and I took the 12 hour drive to Chicago the weekend of October 17, 2012. My class reunion was meeting that weekend in Chicago at the Navy Pier. My friend, who we are going to call "Rich," and I rode around Gary and Chicago before heading over to Price's mom's house, I wanted to make sure I saw Price's mom and aunt before I left Chicago.

Let me quite lying, I really wanted them to see how I stepped my game up from being with someone who had nothing to someone who has something. The looks on both their face said enough, Price's aunt let me know by saying, "He is fine as hell I knew you could do better, Sam!" Then she asked Rich what he did for a living.

Rich replied, "I'm a cop and in the military."

Ahe said, "Oh!" I laughed!

His aunt said, "Have you saw Price yet?" I told her no and that was my next stop. She said, "He is going to be mad at you." We laughed and she called him. She passed me the phone after he picked up, I told Price I was in town and he invited me to come over to smoke at his crib. Price had his own apartment on the Southside of Chicago. He gave me the address and we headed out.

We pulled up I called Price to come out because it looked like the building was secure and I needed access to get inside. Not only did Price come out but Luciano came out behind him. I was kind of irritated and felt betrayed. I had been talking to Luciano the entire ride to Chicago and he knew the plot I was planning.

When they both saw Rich they both had a surprised look on their face. Yes this brother was drop dead, model-fine, 6 feet tall, ripped for the GOD's, goatee, caramel skin tone, (same as Price) real good hair, with a low cut fade, a deep Baltimore accent, and a swag out of this world, his swag spoke for him just sitting in my car. Price stopped in his tracks and told us to come in and Luciano came to the car and immediately introduced himself to Rich. Luciano and Rich shook hands and we all proceeded to go into the apartment.

It felt weird walking into Prices place. I hadn't seen him in some time and we weren't talking like that, it had only been a month since we started communicating. Before that we were constantly into it because his side pieces kept hitting me up on Facebook telling me to, "Leave their man alone!" **Blank Stare** I should have told them all, "Don't feel special boo, he cheats on all his boyfriends and even his husband," but I took the high road.

This dude could not stop lying to his dates, trying to get them to have a reason to think there was a possibility we even had a chance. I was trying to put my feelings of being angry to the side. Before I left to come to Chicago I received a message on Tagged from one of the guys who tried to kill me in Dallas.

The message read, "How did you like that ass whopping? Betta be glad the gun jammed!" That shit scared the fuck out of me and pissed me off at the same time. There was only a picture of some white jeans someone had on but the picture only showed their legs in the jeans. I thought it could have been Price playing a trick or it could have really been one of the guys, either way I put all those feelings to the side to get this divorce.

While in Price's Kitchen Price and Rich started rolling blunts, I asked Price to grab me a $20 sack of weed before I got there. I'm quite sure he pinched some from my sack. **All Tea No Shade** While that was going on Luciano kept asking Rich questions about us, "How long ya'll been together, you really like my friend, ya'll stay together?" I had to tell Luciano to shut up, Price got pissed by his questioning and told him to leave.

Luciano got pissed at Price and said, "How you gone put me out and I just paid your rent, nicca I bought this table, I bought these dishes and your damn groceries and you're going to put me out?!" Luciano left after Price gave him a look. This dude still had his pieces in check and his pieces were still taking care of him. While they were going back and forth Rich and I were rubbing on each other's thighs, we kissed and were whispering to each other.

I only did it to piss Price off and show him I'd moved on but thinking back that was a bad mistake! After we were done smoking Price said he was tired and would catch us in the morning to go to the Daley Center. I said good-bye Rich didn't say anything and didn't shake Price hand when Price extended his. Not even an hour passed when Price called and said he was not going to the court house and not going to sign anything! Dirty Bitch!

My third attempt was in South Carolina on January 23, 2015. I decided the third time was going to be the charm and I was going to do it the "illegal way." My bestie lived in South Carolina and the state just passed the law for "Gay Marriage." Georgia still hadn't passed their law for Gay marriage and it wasn't even recognized. Timothy only lived two and half hours away and I drove there and started the process.

I received my ID and used Timothy's address as a place of residency. I spoke to a lawyer and was ready to go I gave the lawyer Price's information so he could be served. The lawyer was going to take my case "Pro Bono." He wanted the publicity of being the first to do a "Gay Divorce" in the state of South Carolina. We were not sure if it was going to be the first in the history of the United States but we wanted to give it a go. The first question the lawyer asked me was "Have Price and I had sex, spent the night together or eaten dinner together in the last year." Apparently if I had said yes to any of this the lawyer could not go through with the divorce.

Price and I didn't have any children and no property to split so the divorce should go smoothly. The lawyer contacted Price, Price told him in order for him to go through with the divorce he wanted half of the properties or I could sell them and give him half of the money and he wanted half of the profits from my books too. The lawyer called me back and told me and I told him I didn't have any of the properties and they were in foreclosure. The lawyer told me to wait until everything was complete then contact him afterwards. Once again I was pissed. The devil was surly having his way with me and the devil was Price!

My fourth attempt was here in Georgia on August 3, 2015 after Gay Marriage became legal in the state. This date was ironic it was the day of Price birthday and the actual day before we were married August 4, 2008. I wanted this to be over with badly, I hit many snags because Price didn't live in Georgia. I hope I was not going to be stuck with this bastard forever. I prayed we didn't hit the 10 year mark being married and we weren't even together.

The good memories of sex with Price have faded away the bad ones remain. I don't really remember the depth of our sex life now. Generally you can remember someone you had really good bomb sex with and I know that was one reason why I honestly fell in love with him. I just know the sex was good sometimes and bad others.

The memories I do remember include when he infected me with HIV and the very last time we had sex in September of 2010 during the whole "Dallas Texas debacle." I knew that day we were done sexually because I didn't get aroused.

I have never had a problem admitting when I was wrong like this time when I married Price. I learned some people only pursue you to take you back. Price was an arrogant gas bag. You can't put lipstick on a pig and call it a person it's still a pig! I knew I was dancing with the devil wearing sheep's clothing after a while I just choose to see the good in him. I thought my good energy would have brought the devil out of him.

The knife Price stuck in my back became useful when it came time to cut my ties with him. It's sad because I've written both books, *Eyes With Out A Face* and *How It All Happened*, stating

Price was still in the same place where I met him. Unfortunately, seven years later and another book Price is still in that same place, lying cheating and using every lover he gets to get ahead but still in the same place. I've learned people like Price only lie on days that end in y! I just wished I treated myself the same way I treated Price. More importantly I learned the only pain that last forever is death.

* * * * *

My best friend loves me. The bestie treated me to an all-expense paid trip to New Orleans for my birthday. The only catch my car needed to be driven and I was cool with that. December 11, 2015 we headed on the six-hour drive to New Orleans. Timothy drove to me as usual and then we hit the road it was just a weekend trip and we were returning on Sunday. My home girl Marilyn from Minnesota lived in New Orleans and was going to be our tour guide.

I loved how Timothy always had the best accommodations ready for us he reminded me so much of Jonathan. We stayed at none other than the Marriott in Metairie New Orleans Timothy had the Presidential suite with the lake view. YYYAAAASSSSS BITCH WE'RE HERE! I planned to sow my royal oats while there. **Baby** In my New Orleans voice!

We arrived in New Orleans at 7 a.m. and tried to check into the hotel but it was too early check-in wasn't until 10am. The lady at the front desk took Timothy's phone number and told him she would call if the room became available sooner.

Timothy and I decided to ride around and get breakfast until we receive the call. It wasn't so bad, it was early and we weren't sleepy, it was just a 6 hour drive and we made in five hours. I called

Marilyn before she went to work to let her know we were there. Marilyn said she got off work at 4 p.m. and would be ready to hit the town.

I was ready all I wanted to do was eat some seafood, seafood everything I wanted seafood gumbo, shrimp, crab, calamari and those famous crawfish I've never had. Crawfish and seafood gumbo were the only things I really wanted while I was in New Orleans. The whole time, once we entered the city limits, of New Orleans my Jack'd was going crazy.

There were so many fine men in the area some men were Creole I'd never even come in contact with a Creole person to my knowledge. My mother's mom's people were Creole I never met them. I heard Creole people can put a spell on you and my ass was scared every time a Creole dude viewed my page. **It had Creole in the race section of their profile**

We stopped at this restaurant and when we walked in everyone turned and looked at us. There was only 1 table available and it was next to the bathroom. Did I mention everyone in the restaurant was white and older?! The waitress said, "Morning have a seat and I'll be right with you!" After everyone else was done looking at us like we were about to rob the place an elderly white man tried to give us the stare down.

Timothy starred him right back on down I said, "Chile let's go ain't nobody got time to be going to jail out of town and on my birthday weekend!" We got out of there but not before I stared his old racist ass down while we were walking out the door. Some of the other restaurants we rode passed had an old look to them and I didn't want to eat in a place that looked bad, presentation was everything. We ended up eating at the Waffle House everything else either didn't look right or was closed.

Soon as we finished eating and were about to pay our bill the lady from the hotel called and said our room was ready. We headed back to the hotel and the entire ride there I was chatting with some guy named Brandon. Brandon was sexy, had dreads, brown skin, 5'9, was 160 pounds and 28 years old from his profile. What attracted me to Brandon was he looked very masculine in all of his pictures and even the different pictures he texted me.

We walked in the hotel room and were amazed, it was beautiful everything was modern from our bed, to the couches and the bathroom design, the staff was even nice. The lady at the front desk called Timothy after we'd been in the room for a few minutes. She wanted to make sure if we needed anything, what so ever, we call at any time, now that's was the kind of service I liked and that's what I call hospitality.

We tried to take a nap but were too excited. We both had friends who stayed there and we wanted to go see them and do everything else. We only had a day and a half before we needed to get back on the road so we started getting ready to head back out to the city after we showered and got dressed.

Marilyn was going to be off work in a couple of hours. We ate again at the River Walk next to the pier, the scene was magnificent, and the water was tranquil. After we finished we walked through the River Walk, the mall was right there Marilyn called a little later and we headed to her place.

It was nice seeing Marilyn I hadn't seen her since May when she came to Atlanta for my graduation party she was just like a mother figure to me and a good friend. We hugged, had drinks while we all got caught up. Before we knew it it was after 10 p.m. We all headed to Bourbon Street to get drunk and party all night long.

Marilyn had us trying all type of drinks Timothy has a high tolerance for alcohol and my tolerance was low I wasn't driving so I got white boy wasted. I wanted to enjoy myself with my friends in a new setting, no due dates, no homework, no issues, no drama, life was great! We ended the night about 2 a.m. and headed back to the hotel after we droppedMarilyn off.

Saturday morning we made sure to get up at 7 a.m., the hotel was serving free breakfast and it was a full breakfast we were not going to miss a free full breakfast! We piled our plates high and brought the food back to the room. After we ate we passed back out. Marilyn called to wake us up to see what time we were getting together we were going to see some of our friends and go out to eat afterwards. I had a date with Brandon later that night so we got up right away. **Side Stare**

I was supposed to see my home girl Jennifer from back home in Gary she lived in Baton Rouge and was going to drive down and Timothy was going to see his friend Shawn. Jennifer never answered her phone so we went to Timothy's friend. We ended up staying there over 2 hours with them talking and catching up. He and his wife are cool, Timothy knew Shawn's mother and watched him grow up from a child and it felt like I knew them too.

We left there and headed to Marilyn's, she took us around town again and we saw some different places. I was amazed at this one cemetery it was kind of creepy but it was very intriguing with all mausoleums. Everything was above ground I didn't see one head stone on the ground. Marilyn also took us around some flooded areas I felt bad for the city and everyone who lost their lives, their families and everyone else affected by Hurricane Katrina. **RIP to the victims and their families*

It was almost midnight and we were lit, we had stopped at Bourbon Street again and had a few drinks. We bar hoped and did a couple of videos and posted them to Facebook. Most of the bars were like clubs they actually were clubs with in and out access. You could even bring your drink in from another club on the strip. They were playing Michael Jackson karaoke and we sang our little drunken hearts out, afterwards it was time to go, my date was waiting!

Brandon was calling me all day he was eager to meet up I believe it was because I was a new face in a new place. He kept my attention he stated right away he was HIV positive my Jack'd profile had that I was HIV positive. He lived alone, had a car and a job but he was not in Atlanta I knew this would just be a hook up for the weekend it couldn't be anything more my feelings were turned off, we all grown!

Brandon met me at the hotel around 2 a.m. I had him come there I didn't want to drive to him and I wanted him to meet Timothy he looked like a thug and I didn't want to get robbed or car jacked in a different state. Brandon was a sweet heart we all had a quick conversation while Timothy grilled him and got this man's address, a picture of his driver's license and where he worked. Timothy walked us outside and took a picture of his car and license plate my best friend doesn't play!

The ride to Brandon's house felt like I knew him already he drove an Altima and he was driving slow rubbing on my thigh the entire ride he lived downtown by the Superdome. We walked through the door and he started stripping LAWD I could have fainted. This man's body was every got damn thing! In my mind I just kept thinking "only if he lived in Atlanta!"

After smoking two blunts we hit the shower and by this time it was 4 a.m. and he had to be at work at 9 a.m. I felt like an entrée the way Brandon had me in the shower. We went from the shower to the living room to the bedroom to the patio outside that opened from his bedroom on the second floor. That man had his way with me and I loved every motherfucking minute of it! By the time we were done it was close to 8 a.m. we showered and he drove me back to the hotel.

The entire ride back I didn't say much. Brandon asked if I was okay I told him I was I just was in my thoughts and feelings. He asked did he do something wrong and I told him no. I actually was in my feelings because I had been having sexual relations with Clinton and I felt like I was cheating although we were not together. I knew Clinton loved me with all his heart and I felt like I had betrayed him in the worst way by cheating.

I walked through the hotel door and immediately called Clinton I felt bad and I was on a guilt trip. Clinton asked if he could go with us to New Orleans but I told him no because it was just going to be Timothy and I. I told him what I did with Brandon I could hear the disappointment in his voice. Clinton told me, "You feel guilty because you know where my heart is and I know you feel something if you didn't you wouldn't be on the phone with me right now telling me this!" He was so right!

Clinton told me it was cool and he would see me when I got home I felt good after hanging up with him. Marilyn called soon as I hung up with Clinton she was ready to go out to breakfast. Timothy and I planned on leaving at noon I didn't need to shower but I did anyway. We checked out of the hotel grabbed our set of towels and headed to Marilyn's. After we ate breakfast we headed back to Marilyn's she packed up some things for us to take back home.

She had given us all kinds of candles and beads she gave me a set of vases, some hanging pictures and some smell goods and gave Timothy a big mirror I wanted and some hanging pictures. I was going to miss New Orleans that weekend trip was unforgettable but I was going to miss my dear friend Marilyn even more. She promised to come down May 2017 for my graduation. We all hugged and kissed before Timothy and I hit the highway back to Atlanta.

* * * * *

Soon as I came back home #26 surprised me and came into town, we went out to eat and spent the night together. After #26 left Clinton and I ended up going out to dinner and spending the night together. I was honestly torn between the two people who didn't know about each other. I felt bad; I knew karma was right around the corner.

I couldn't believe it, was a week right after my birthday I ended up in the hospital karma came quickly.

My friends Onsemious, Cody and Jen were coming over, we planned to go to Lenox to do some Christmas shopping it was 3 days before Christmas and we knew the mall was going to be mad packed.

Early morning on December 22, my friends met up at my house around 9 a.m. Cody and I decided to ride with Jen being she'd just bought a new car I didn't want to drive and Cody came from across town and didn't want to drive either. Onsemious called me into the bedroom and said, "Bro don't let her drive I passed her on the highway coming here and she looked scared bro!" I blew him off. I thought he was being funny.

Onsemious stayed behind at my house Cody and I left out with Jen. We all got in the car with her, I was in the front and Cody sat behind me. Jen had a cute 2014 Toyota Camry it was a blue 4door. We got on the highway a couple of blocks from my house. I was on my phone on Facebook, Cody had his Beats by Dre on because Jen put in her latest Mary J. Blige cd, this girl knows she loves her some Mary J. Blige.

Next, all I heard was a scream and when I looked up I saw the tail end of the semi-truck on the left side of us. We were merging onto the highway and next we were doing 360's across the highway. All I could see were cars and trucks coming towards us then us heading in the right direction along with traffic and cars and trucks headed towards us about 3 times and lots of smoke inside the car from the tires burning.

We ended up against the center median with the driver side pinned against the wall facing oncoming traffic it was crazy and scary at the same time. After coming to I was on top of Cody in the back seat with my head at his feet and my feet at his head with my lower right side in his face. Cody was unconscious and bleeding from his mouth Jen was good just scared and dazed.

People were trying to get us out of the car. Traffic was stopped from what I could see. When the ambulance arrived Cody came to, I only realized once I got out of the car Cody's tooth was knocked out. He bit me below my butt and I pissed my pants somewhere in the process.

The paramedics loaded us into two separate ambulances, Jen rode with me I was trying to ride with Cody I felt he needed the most attention. On the ride to the hospital I asked Jen what the hell happened. Jen said as she was merging onto the highway, a car was in front and a car was on the side of the semi-truck, the semi-truck couldn't merge over. She said a car was coming behind her fast and she sped up and hit the tail corner of the semi-truck and next thing she knew she was spinning.

Onsemious was calling our phones ever since the accident. I didn't answer until after Jen told me what happened. I told him what happened and what hospital we were going to. He was there by the time we were being wheeled in. I lived not even 10 minutes from the hospital I told the ambulance driver he was my brother. Onsemious had tears in his eyes I could tell he knew it was bad because I told him Cody was in the ambulance behind us and he just came to.

Jen was being questioned by the police as soon as the ambulance doors opened. Onsemious bent down and hugged me, when we got into the hospital room the tears started falling from his eyes. Onsemious said, "Bro I told you not to ride with her because she looked scared as fuck on the highway!"

I said, "If you would have said the scared as fuck part I would have listened." We laughed a little but not too much I was in pain.

Cody ended up staying in the hospital for two days, lost a tooth and had to get stitches on his lower lip. I was released after about six hours and required six stiches below my butt. My girl Jen got a ticket for reckless driving, speeding and went to jail for not having car insurance.

I was pissed. I was going to have to cover my own hospital bill. I wasn't going to sue her and I was sad my girl was going to jail. I was thankful we all survived. The car accident could have killed any of us or all of us. Once again, GOD said it wasn't my time!

CHAPTER 14

IT WASN'T BY CHANCE

Finally it was all coming together I know the saying, "GOD brings people into your life for a reason, season and a lifetime." By this time I realized why I met everyone within my life I found me in the process of trying to find them. At some points I lost myself and in the end I found myself and I was truly happy with the results.

I learned if GOD allowed me to lose it, then HE's going to replace it with something better! My heart is at ease knowing what was meant for me will never miss me and what misses me was never meant for me. You are always supposed to treat people right you never know what's in store for you. When your cup runneth over, pour some in someone else's cup.

I was in the middle of writing this book, going to school, traveling, in a relationship, socializing with friends, making sure my priorities were in order, being spiritual, keeping in contact with family and friends all while trying to network to build up my Youth Center.

When KB passed away September 2, 2015 it made me look at myself as well as my circle of friends. I noticed how my friendships flourished I cherished everyone within my company. Timothy came into my life as we both were going through a terrible break up. I was breaking up with Price and he was breaking up with Terry. We both were used in those relationships and learned our value through each other.

TaQuan is my male gay mentor he came into my life to show me anything was possible. David, TaQuan's fiancé, was me in every way, we thought alike I could tell what he was thinking at times he was what I wanted to be when I was with Price, laid back and relaxed. Kevin and Quinton were a support system in my time of need. No matter what we went through they were still there for me. Moe, George and Jermeal were all younger and I was a mentor to them in my mind. I constantly told them of my mistakes so they knew what routes not to take.

Tika put me in my place along with TaQuan, they were friends that brought me back if I stepped outside of my body. They gave me tough love whether I liked it or not, at times I needed that! Franda is my mentor here in Atlanta she stepped in when my sister was busy. Pearl is like a big sister who watches out for me along with Diane, they both are always on the lookout for ways of helping me promote my mission. Miyasha and Damion came into my life to let me know I can get knocked down at any moment and I still have to get right back up!

Keisha is someone here in Atlanta who knew me from way back when she was my high school class mate and close friend she knew me better than anyone other than Tiffanie and Angela. I've known Tiffanie since I was 13 years old my first job was working at her father's liquor store and candy shop called "Papa Adams."

Angela is my best friend she has been my best friend since we were 14 years old. In our 23 years of friendship, we've only had one falling out. I learned true friends can go through it and still be the best of friends after it. I know without Angela and Keisha may she rest in peace I know I would not be here. Angela is my best friend indeed and I love her.

Molly was placed in my life to show me what true real friends are she was my ex-husbands close friend and told me he was cheating while we were still together. She loved me so much she became one of my best friends. I love her for her honesty and for telling me my worth when I didn't even know it.

Marilyn was a mother figure I needed she was there since I was 22 years old. She loved me like I was her own child but conversed with me as a friend. #26 and #14 both came into my life to let me know it was possible for me to love again after being broken hearted. I've learned friendship isn't about whom you've known the longest it's about who walked into your life and said, "I'm here for you" and proved it.

Nate' Billingsley-Walton and I attended Roosevelt High School together, she graduated class of 1998. I witnessed her growth on Facebook, she went through a bad relationship, bounced back, finished school with a Bachelor's degree, became a teacher, got married in a new relationship and has 2 children. Nate' is a free spirited kind person, she has no idea how much I love and admire her! When I think of her tears come to my eyes she's my inspiration, determination and motivation.

My naughty publisher, my seven molesters, two second cousins who had sex with me, Bob my mother's boyfriend, Kim the neighborhood whore, the women and men who paid me for sex, the hook ups, the dating scene and Price were nothing more than mere lessons. These people were not a waste of time at all, they were all blessings. I learned from them ignorant people have been around for a long time and they're not going anywhere any time soon.

*****

I flew out to California May 31 for my niece Alexus' graduation. My flight left at 10:30 a.m. I got to the airport around eight to avoid the long lines I made it through security very quick. It felt weird riding in the airplane we had turbulence and I was scared as shit! Although I've been through turbulence before but for some reason this time I was a nervous wreck it didn't help the fact I kept thinking about the terrorist blowing up the plane. **Don't Judge Me** Malaysia flight MH370 and Egypt Air flight 804 both going missing had me worried but like always I fell asleep in the air with my mouth wide open.

I hadn't been to California nor seen my sister and her family in 6 years. The last time I was there I was really in a bad place in my life I was going through the break up with Price. Coming here now put everything in perspective. I had a chance to look back where I was then and look at life today and I know there is a GOD!

I have been to California a total of 6 times within my life with two of those times on bad terms. I was married in San Francisco August 4, 2008 I didn't see my sister that time. My very first time meeting my niece Alexus was when my sister's dad passed away in 1999 they came to the funeral in Gary, Alexus was a baby just 1 year old. I drove down from Minnesota to Gary for the funeral. At that point I hadn't seen my sister since 1994 when she lived with my dad, brother and me for a very short period of time.

During the Mexico trip in 2001 Jonathan and I were stranded due to 9/11. We took four flights from Mexico only to land in Tijuana we walked across the border into California. My sister, her husband and baby Alexus met us outside of customs. We stayed with them over night our flights were scheduled to depart the next morning.

May 2009 Price, my brother, his ex-wife Tonya and I went to California for my sister's graduation. My mother purchased my brother and his wife tickets instead of purchasing her own she felt she didn't need to come because her children were all going to be together. **Blank Stare** We all stayed in the same hotel I rented the rental car for us. My sister rented a limousine and we rode with her to her graduation.

The next time I went to California I moved there. Price and I broke up 2010. I left for California April 21. I lived with my sister and her family from April 22 to July 31, before moving back like a dumb ass to Dallas, Texas.

Six years later I was back in California and this time for a damn good reason. My niece Alexus was graduating from high school I wasn't going to miss that for nothing in the world. I went to the twin's graduation but didn't make it on time. I had to go to Alexus' graduation I picked my niece graduation over my grandma's party with no hesitation. I didn't grow up with my sister nor with my nieces I wanted to make sure I was a part of every accomplishment in my nieces lives. My niece Alexus is my spitting image twin. I really could have been her father. Alexus and my nephew DeAndre are my twins they look just like me.

I stayed with my sister although my trip was short from Tuesday to Thursday it was the quality of time spent not the quantity of days I was there. We did many things from sitting around talking the first night to my sister driving me around to show me all the new homes in her area. They were beautiful I was proud of my sister considering our backgrounds.

The next day was graduation day my niece looked amazing and like the female version of me. I met my in laws, sisters' friends, my niece's friends and my niece Alexus boyfriend. My sister rented a limo and we rode around town after the graduation. My niece was playing songs from her phone and we all sang. Everyone met back at my sister's house and we went to "Barona Resort & Casino" they have a buffet.

After returning from the buffet and after everything was over, it was about 2 p.m. we all sat in the living room from 2 p.m. to midnight talking, watching TV and enjoying our time together. Of course I was hungry, I was always hungry since my braces were taken out. My sister's best friend LaTeace took me to Wing Stop, she's mad cool and very pretty I've known her now for 6 years. The next morning my sister took me back to the airport around 5:30am, my flight left at 7:30. I talked to my sister on the phone until I sat in my seat on the plane. The love I have for my sister is a love that can't even be described. My sister is my everything.

I landed back at Hartsfield-Jackson Atlanta International airport Clinton picked me up. We were supposed to jump on the road and leave for Delaware soon as I got into the car. My baby decided to work instead of taking the day off instead and was tired. I had jet lag so we went home and went to sleep first we didn't end up leaving until 4am.

I road with Clinton plenty of times and out of town but he makes me nervous from his driving sometimes. One time he switched lanes very fast and the car felt like it was about to go off the road. A couple of times he's pumped on the breaks so hard and

I rose up out of my seat. His driving scared the shit out of me but his driving record is "squeaky clean." He has the better insurance rate too I switched insurance companies to get added to his policy. **Side Stare** After a while, eventually I would fall asleep with my mouth wide open.

Clinton and I pulled into the hotel parking lot a little after 7 p.m. The closer we got to the hotel exit slowing down I began to see cotton flying in the air. This was the first time in my life I ever seen cotton up close it was astonishing. His sister and her fiancé just made it to the hotel a few minutes ahead of us the love and bond they have is in impeccable.

We couldn't get out the car quick enough before his sister ran up to hug him it reminded me of my sister and me. After she hugged Clinton his sister gave me a hug and said, "It's finally nice to meet after speaking with you and hearing so much about you from my brother, it's great to put a face with the voice I've been speaking with for months." She was so sweet.

We all showered and headed to their mother's house for dinner Clinton's mom was cooking dinner for the family. I was nervous I had been talking to Clinton's mom for a couple of months on the phone. When pulled up my jitters went away I still couldn't believe I was about to meet his mom and the rest of the family!

Soon as we walked through the door of his mother's home she hugged me immediately she thanked me for loving her son and said welcome to our family. She said, "Call me Momma Dee!" Momma Dee put me at ease and made me feel comfortable right away. She hugged her children and her son in-law to be, Clinton's sister is engaged. Within a few minutes Clinton's mom headed outside and Clinton told me to follow her, looking lost I followed behind her.

Once out the door she thanked me again for loving her son. She said he had been through a lot with his ex-boyfriend she was thankful her son was finally happy. She told me her son needs lots of attention and I agreed we both laughed hard. She told me a little about her life and I told her a little about mine.

Momma Dee congratulated me on my books and what I was trying to accomplish to help others. She also apologized for her father's behavior Clinton told her what his grandfather said when he first met me. My baby's mom is the truth!

After we were done talking, well after the mosquitoes ate us up, we couldn't take it anymore, we went back into the house and ate dinner and talked at the dinner table like a family! While we were eating and talking, a couple of bae friends he grew up with came by to see him it was cool watching their interactions, he knew his friends since childhood.

I woke up the next morning to a call from my father. My father wanted to make sure I was happy he said he woke up with me on his mind and wanted to check in on his son. My dad had been checking up on me quite often since he came down to Atlanta for my graduation. I see my speech from my graduation book release party really worked, I prayed hard for it.

I told my dad I was good and in Delaware visiting and meeting Clinton's family. Before we hung up my dad said, "Make sure you tell that young man I said hello he also told me don't take no wooden nickels they may burn but you can't spend them." My dad was always throwing out little tidbits of life lessons. I love that man!

After we were dressed we headed to New Jersey so Clinton could meet my friends TaQuan and David. We crossed over the Delaware Memorial Bridge while we were singing and in a happy place. Bae mom called and told him what time dinner would be served and be sure to be back there around that time. I loved the time we spent with Momma Dee and her cooking too. **Smiles Hard**

We made it to TaQuan and David's after 1 p.m. TaQuan brought some blue crabs, crab legs, shrimp and potatoes. He wanted to have a little crab boil and sip wine while they meet and converse with the new love of my life. We all ate, drank and talked. TaQuan made a special family seasoning to dip the crab and shrimps in. Everything was just so perfect it seemed if I were living in a fairy tale dream until Brooklyn peed on their carpet. **Pissed Off Stare**

The sky turned gray with clouds, we decided to head back to Delaware around 6:30 p.m. it was starting to rain and traffic was already bad. Momma Dee said dinner was at 9 p.m. Clinton's sister and her fiancé went to New York she visited her family and her dad they left out an hour prior to us.

Between the 14 hours it took to get from Atlanta to Delaware, walking the dogs and bathroom breaks I began to value my relationship so much more. Price showed me a lot I'm thankful for today in my relationship with Clinton. For one, with my relationship I'm a slut not a whore meaning I'll try anything but not anyone. We kept no secrets we had the passcodes to our phones set the same not that we needed to go into each phones. We talked about everything there is no holding back and no attitudes.

I learned to talk my issues out rather than being silent carrying around an attitude I learned to appreciate everything Clinton brought to the table. More importantly living in Atlanta I learned it's nothing sexier than someone who can face temptation and have the level of maturity to say this isn't worth losing what I have.

On the road back to Delaware we ran into the rainstorm ended up stopping for gas and snacks at the gas station in New Jersey I was on my fat boy mode. I was surprised at the fact you couldn't pump your own gas in parts of New Jersey what was that all about? Getting back on the road we ran into Clinton's sister. It was ironic we're driving listening to the radio and Clinton says, "Look there is my sister" it was unbelievable to be at the exact spot at the exact same time.

We made it back to Momma Dee's house on time. Momma Dee and I went back outside to talk she was telling me how the family is from Jamaica, Panama, Barbados, Puerto Rico and most of them moved to New York. She loves her family and wanted more family gatherings. Momma Dee told me Clinton needs someone to push him, she loved all of her children and glad they were 18 and up with significant others accept the 18 year old. We ate dinner then headed back to the hotel to get some sleep we had a long day ahead of us.

Sunday was graduation day for Clinton's baby brother. Clinton and his sister met their niece Aniah for the first time she was only 8 days old. Momma Dee was cooking breakfast for everyone we were all rushing to get to the graduation ceremony and we took our breakfast to go. Clinton and I drove his little brother to his graduation and Clinton did 90 mph all the way there, he was graduating from the "Bob Carpenter Center" and it was 30 minutes away from their house.

Momma Dee and the rest of the family left shortly behind us the graduation started at 1 p.m. we arrived at 12:40. It felt good being in the presence of Clinton's family and seeing another one of our youth graduating heading to the next phase of their life. Clinton's little brother was going off to college with a full scholarship. He is going to be playing football and going to school to become an engineer.

We went and visited some of Clinton's close friends before heading back to his mom's house after the ceremony. When we made it back to Clinton's mom's his step dad wanted everyone to take a family picture. Momma Dee called me from inside to come outside to get in the picture. She said you're family now baby come on and get in this picture which made me feel good and loved.

We took a couple of pictures with different poses and went back in. Momma Dee told everyone she cooked us all a pineapple upside down cake it was to be split with his sister, the other siblings and us. We all said our goodbyes and hugged each other. Momma Dee hugged me a lot she thanked me for loving her son hoped and wished for us the best and we jumped on the road back to Atlanta it was after 7 p.m. At the end of the day Clinton has my back and I have his I am not saying this loosely. We have now known each other a little over a full year. I wouldn't trade him even if he had a twin.

*****

Brooklyn and Lacey are our babies I love them so much. I have to take all the credit for spoiling them especially Lacey. She is the baby and the little one I would hold and cradle her. She would either fall asleep close next to me, on my back, or on my lap. I had my fair share of times of being upset at them too. One day someone came and knocked on the door. Clinton told me over and over again to put them into the room if someone is knocking at the door because they will run out they are used to living in a house with a fenced in yard.

When I heard someone knocking at the door I told them to get back, I opened the door no one was there and they flew out! I caught Lacey right away but I couldn't catch Brooklyn for shit. We lived on the third floor at the time I jumped from the third floor to the second floor. I almost broke my damn knee I fell to the ground I couldn't get back up I had to catch my damn breath. My neighbor ended up catching Brooklyn and bringing him to me thank GOD someone was there. Clinton was going to have one less dog. **Serious Blank Stare**

They both act a fool when a cat comes around and it's funny they be barking and trying to chase the cat while on leashes. Brooklyn cries every time he goes into the cage at night when it's time to go to sleep. Clinton has to yell at him to lay down every night I'll be in the bed laughing silently. Not to mention one day during a rain storm he was stuck in the couch before when no one was home, he hates thunder. I didn't put them in the cage when I left I hate for them babies to be caged up. Then we have the famous Ms. Lacey who tears up every bed they get. I don't know what the hell her problem is she scratches the bed up something fierce before laying down. One day the dogs were on the balcony and Brooklyn fell off. We went searching for him in the pouring rain. He was okay but Clinton was devastated and I saw it in his eyes.

*****

I was thinking of all types of ways to get my mission and story out to the public I thought about doing videos of things I went through. I did videos about my petition to inform people to sign it, and video's about determination, the death threats I've received, coping skills, bullying, domestic violence, rape, AIDS/HIV, rejection, why we as a people are divided, statutory rape, promiscuous sex and racism. I even started the process to have a 501 C3 for a youth center.

My application for my youth center needed more information from the IRS when I first submitted it I filled out "one wrong form" and it was declined. The examiner called right away informing me she was mailing out an amendment and to follow the instructions in order to precede with the process.

Next step was heading down to the Secretary of State (SOS). I started the process on May 3, and my application was rejected on May 31 for the information already on my application I went back the next day to fill out the correct form. My application was rejected a total of three times before it finally went through on June 8, 2016. It was approved on June 10 from the (SOS). The devil was trying me but GOD showed up and showed out because this had to be done!

My examiner from the IRS called me the following Monday asking for me to fax her my approval from the SOS. After faxing her the information I called and left a voicemail letting her know I submitted the request. After the IRS approved my application I received my documentation on July 5, 2016. I wrote up my GoFundMe account information to open the doors for people to donate and help me get my organization going. I'm including the account information in this book to allow each of you the opportunity to assist me as well.

http://www.gofundme.com/youthcenter4s-a-m

I am now living out my goal to provide understanding and healing to all who have been abused, Enough Is Enough! I wanted to make sure I was divorced before everything I envisioned got off the ground. I am well on my way to seeing my dreams and goals come true. I didn't want Price thinking he was entitled to shit!

I received Price's phone number from a good source. I called him and we spoke for a brief minute. I asked him if I could have his address to mail him the divorce papers. Price said, "We're not divorced yet I just knew you would find a sneaky way to take care of that," while laughing. I wasn't laughing at all. I told him if he would have gone to the court house years ago while I was in Chicago we would have been divorced. Rat bastard didn't know I tried doing it the "illegal way" but GOD wanted it done the right way.

This bitch had the nerve to say, "So you mean to tell me we have been married for 8 years next month we might as well just stay married then!" I said, "We have been separated longer than we were married." Price knew about the "California Law" if we were married for 10 years he automatically gets half of everything I own. I asked him for his address again and he gave it to me but not without saying, "This is ironic I just went to Walgreens today and had our wedding picture blown up and it's in my living room!"

I laughed, said, "Thank you, aight bro," and hung up.

I mailed the divorce application to the Sheriff's Office located inside of the "Daley Center" in Chicago, Illinois the very next day on July 5, 2016 the exact same day I received the final paper work for my Youth Center! The devil still tried me, I had court on July 19 and since Price hadn't been served as of that date the judge dismissed the case. She told me once Price was served to file a "MOTION FOR RELIEF FROM JUDGMENT OR FOR RECONSIDERATION."

I went to the "Family Law office" in the court building and attained all the paperwork I needed to file the motion I filled everything out and waited. Look at GOD, Price was finally served on

July 20, 2016 at 4:04 p.m. at his home. The very next day I went back to the courts and filed the motion! My motion was granted on Price's birthday August 3!

I received the "NOTICE OF FINAL HEARING" on August 22 and immediately sent Price a certified copy, I had to notify him! I couldn't believe Price refused to sign the papers that notified him of the divorce court date. Oh well, if he came or not we were still getting this damn divorce! I posted the paper to Facebook with, "Save The Date … Breaking Every Chain!"

* * * * *

During Atlanta's Annual Pride September 1-5, Pearl flew in from Dallas Texas, George flew in from Houston, and Jermeal flew in from Chicago. Kevin, Sharon, Dexter, Elliot, Norman, Brandon, Victor, Clinton and I kicked it from Thursday to Monday during Pride here in ATL. We had a dinner and card party on Tuesday at our place.

Wednesday September 7th we celebrated Clinton's Birthday with a surprise Birthday dinner Kevin planned for me at "Mary Mac's Tea Room." Miyasha rode with Clinton and I to Mary Mac's Tea Room, Kevin, Franda, Keisha, Sharon, Victor, Norman, his friend Isaiah were there waiting for us to arrive. Clinton's best friend Will arrived later after he got off work. After we were done eating we went over to Clinton's other best friend Todd's house for drinks, the night was amazing.

Angela, my best friend since we were 14 years old in high school, came and stayed with me for the weekend of September 11th. I've known Angela now for 23 years. Her friends from Gary and Indianapolis came to Atlanta to celebrate one of their birthdays. We talked every night after she came back from the club until 5 or 6 in the morning. We had nothing but good times from talking, laughing and reminiscing.

The next day I sent my books to Stacy. A close friend of mine gave me Stacy Whitt's address in Minnesota and his phone number. I sent him and his fiancé Donita Smith both copies of my books, *Eyes Without A Face* and *How It All Happened*. I autographed both copies like I did with the books I mailed to Antonio "Coop" Davis and Maurice "Munk" Moody.

I was taking my power back and gave him evidence being I put his name in both books so he could sue me if he wanted to. I wrote on the envelope "Signed, Sealed and Delivered." The books were delivered on Wednesday at 12:41 p.m. to their mailbox at their Hopkins residence at 1411 Lake St. NE Hopkins, MN 55343.

I then contacted the lead person, Zac, at gangerstvilleradio.com and gave him Stacy's phone number 612-310-0497. I told him to contact Stacy and see if he would come on the radio to do a show with him and I to talk about my allegations against him. STACY DECLINED THE INTERVIEW, HE NEVER RETURNED THE CALL!

I had been waiting on September 19 for six years and two days shy of five months; it couldn't have come any quicker. Price and I were finally getting a Divorce! I post the FINAL DIVORCE DATE on Facebook and captioned it, "Save the date September 19, 2016!"

The night before going to court I couldn't sleep for anything in the world particularly because I was getting over a cold. However it didn't help that I kept thinking about the wrongs Price did to me including almost losing my life for him. My mind is so strong when I fell asleep I ended up dreaming about being in the back seat of my car getting beat all over again which I talked about in my first book, *Eyes Without A Face*.

Samar was on top of me saying Price didn't want him and it was all my fault. When he put the gun to my head and pulled the trigger I jumped out of my sleep. I hadn't been asleep even an hour; I needed this divorce to rid these horrible memories from my mind because I was carrying this ball and chain with me. I sat in bed and tried to change my thoughts to be positive thoughts but it didn't work I couldn't think of anything positive about Price and I. He hurt me to the core and I just wanted out, there was no coming back.

It was time to get up and ready for court, 8:30 a.m. couldn't have come any quicker. My clothes were ironed, my evidence was ready I just needed to shower and be out of the house by 9am. Clinton was already up and getting ready, he slept on the couch the night before I didn't want him catching my cold. On the ride to the court house Clinton asked if I okay I said, "Never better just waiting for this to be over!"

Trying to find parking in the parking garage of the courthouse was impossible all the spaces were filled. When Clinton and I reached the top floor I decided to get out and let him find parking while I went to check-in on time in room 6C. No sooner than I walked into the courtroom the judge called my name on the rooster, after fifteen minutes Clinton walked in.

After the judge heard a few cases in which he sent a man to jail for failure to pay his child support, another man had to pay more child support and give some of the proceeds to his ex-wife from selling an old school vehicle without her permission and another case he dismissed all because he said he follows his "values."

Finally it was my turn to approach the bench and sit in the chair. I sensed a problem with the judge as soon as he called me to approach he snickered after he said Price and I names and said, "Are these two men?"

I replied, "Yes!"

The judge went on to say, "So tell me your story Mr. Holloway you checked one of the boxes with infidelity!"

I pulled out my evidence from my Louie bag and told the judge my soon to be ex-husband had many affairs while we were married. I told him about all the evidence I was prepared to show him to prove my case. After I stated the reason we split was because Price wanted to have a threesome and wanted me to be involved as soon as we moved to Dallas, Texas from Minnesota but I didn't want to. I packed up and moved to California to file for divorce and got caught in my feelings for love, moved back only to allow him to beat me, get arrested, paying to bail him out that same night, just to have him set me up to be robbed, beaten and nearly killed by the same men he wanted me to have the threesome with.

The judge said, "*What?* You don't have to say anymore Mr. Holloway, your divorce is granted!"

Just like that I was finally divorced and Price was now my "EX-WASband!" The feeling I felt was like a weight had been lifted, I was able to breathe better, the ball and chain has been broken.

I was never looking for a Baller, I never wanted anyone to take care of me, I just wanted someone I could build with. Because Price lived a fabulous life while we were married and I took care of him everything I earned and accumulated had to be split, so I gave it all up without giving up one cent! I would never bash nor hate on what once made me happy and smile. I will forever love and cherish our happy memories. Price showed me when someone shows you who they really are the first time BELIEVE THEM!

I couldn't expect adult results from someone with a child-like mind I truly wish Price nothing but the best and fortunately Love Still Wins! The song by Heather Headley, "In my mind," was right and true when she said, "They say if you love something, you've got to let it go. And if it comes back, then it means so much more. Fine if it never does, at least you will know, that it was something you had to go through to grow."

Thursday the same week I met Clinton's Great Aunt Mrs. Judy she came to visit her daughter here in Atlanta from New York. Aunt Judy purchased both of my books, *Eyes Without A Face* and *How It All Happened.* She also purchased a book for her daughter. I had been speaking with her on the phone for about a month before we actually met. Aunt Judy was like Momma Dee very sweet, open, straight forward and funny.

Guest Speaker #VYIWC

After a couple of hours Clinton and I said our good-byes I had to pack for my trip to Houston, Texas where I was a guest speaker for the "Voice Your Invisible Wounds Conference." Aunt Judy's good-bye was, "I got you in the palm of my hand because you're all good with me." I really liked her. Afterwards, my Bae and I got something to eat. I packed and we hit the sack!

Why Did We Meet? — It Wasn't' By Choice

I got up at 4 a.m. to catch my 6:25 a.m. flight to Houston, Texas I only got a few hours of sleep and I was exhausted. Once the plane took off I was sound asleep. It seemed like I dosed off for only a few minutes before we started to descend. My ears had never popped so hard while flying I thought my head was about to explode. I was chewing my gum like crazy and it still didn't, help my ears were plugged for the next 24 hours.

When I got off the plane and was walking toward baggage claim I saw a guy who was holding a sign with my name on it. I was flabbergasted I thought I was taking a shuttle to the hotel where I would be staying. I felt like a celebrity. Pulling up to the "Omni Houston Hotel at Westside" totally blew me away. I felt honored someone thought enough about me to have me as a guest speaker and the accommodations were magnificent I knew this experience was going to be one I would never forget.

After checking into my room on the top floor I went back down stairs to have breakfast. I was on my phone with TaQuan telling him about my beautiful room when I spotted a familiar face, the lady spoke and called me by my name. I spoke back but told TaQuan I didn't know who she was. I stood there in the hotel restaurant waiting to be seated and kept looking at her.

I realized it was Nicole; she lived in Atlanta and was the Chapter President over "Survivors With Voices." Her son was shot and murdered here in Atlanta in 2013 he was only 21 years old and the oldest of her two children. After I realized who she was I quickly went over and hugged her. I let her know I didn't know right away who she was and we laughed. I joined her for breakfast before heading back to my room to catch a nap before the "Meet & Greet" started at 7 p.m.

The "Meet & Greet" started promptly at 7 p.m. I wore the shirt I had worn for my Book Release party with both book covers on it, white jeans and red Jordans (I don't support Michael Jordan he doesn't support his own people. My homeboy Onsemious bought me the Jordans.) and Nicole and I met at the elevators to head into the conference room together. To my surprise our names were on the seats in the front row right in front of the stage.

Before long the Founder of "Survivors With Voices" Alissa arrived and radio host Dawn "The Interviewer" for "The Dr. Dawn Radio Show" which is about no judgment just realness based out of Houston. I felt like I was in a room full of people I knew, some people knew me others knew my story and to some I was a new face. Alissa had my face everywhere from the banner, the flyer, to the projector. I was finally where I wanted to be speaking in my life.

There were many people there; the ambiance was a no judgment zone. People from all walks of life were present and just about everyone had a testimony but not everyone was speaking this was a conference to speak your "Unapologetic Truth" and I was definitely going to speak mine no hold barred. For appetizers there were three different cheeses, crackers, fruits and juice. The food was great. After the "Meet & Greet" was over everyone mingled in the room to get to know each other. When the evening was over Nicole and I walked around the hotel and talked intimately about our lives.

We had to be up at 7 a.m. to get ready the conference that started at 9. Alissa and her husband planned the entire weekend filled with gems to be taken back home to share with others. She started the conference with a monologue of the beginning of her story and what happened to her as a child. Alissa was molested by an uncle her story was very touching. Dr. Dawn then began to interview the guest speakers.

Why Did We Meet? — It Wasn't' By Choice

There were many testimonies from survivors with voices. There was Shauna who was raped three times over a period of 8 hours then shot in the chest above her heart. There was a lady whom had 5 kids and her home burst into flames in the middle of the night, she and some of her children were burned badly and she lost a child who was a twin, a 21 year old college student who was raped by someone she met on campus and there was Nicole, I and others. We were all survivors, some didn't make it but we did, we are the living proof.

For lunch the hotel staff had croissant and bagel ham and turkey sandwiches, spinach salads, chips, fruit, cookies, iced tea and assorted beverages. After lunch there were a few more speakers and a seminar by Lou. Once that part of the conference was over, anyone who was a vendor was able to sell their products, I sold my books. During the conference I met Lauren, which is Alissa's sister. She is just like Alissa, sweet and kind. Lauren, Nicole and I connected right away and spent the rest of the night together. The three of us took the shuttle bus from the hotel to Taco Cabana and conversed the rest of the evening.

The "Red Carpet" started at 6:30 p.m. promptly but we missed it. Nicole and Lauren helped me get dressed and we ended up running late and missing the pictures on the red carpet. I couldn't get my Bowtie right, tightened my vest nor put my cufflinks on. It had been a minute since I wore a 3 piece slim fitted suit with all the fixings. Let me stop lying, my ass ain't never wore a three-piece suit with all the fixings.

Clinton bought my suit, a three-piece navy blue slim fit with cufflinks Bowtie and handkerchief. My sister bought my shoes and socks after I sent her a picture of the shoes I was going to wear with my suit. She said, "I will not let my little brother show up to an event with a suit looking like a million bucks and your shoes look broke. You have to walk into the room and own it!" I told her I was going to walk into the room and own my seat but I actually did walk into the room and own it!

The gala was from 9 to 11 p.m. everyone showed up and showed out for the red carpet we were all casket sharp. Bravo's TV show "Thicker Than Water" featuring "The Tankards" were in attendance along with some other high profile named celebrities. After everyone took pictures and did interviews on the red carpet the songstress "Bre," from Atlanta, sang a song, a ballerina dancer danced to 2 songs, we had dinner and Alissa passed out awards and certificates before telling her story in depth.

After the night was over, I changed clothes and left with George, headed to party at the club. George lived in Houston and wanted to take me out to celebrate. Before we even arrived at the club George was drunk. I guess it didn't help the situation he had 3 more drinks and passed out face forward in the club right in the middle of the dance floor. I had to drive his car back to the hotel and he had to stay because I wouldn't let him drive drunk; hell he couldn't drive anyway.

We made it back to the hotel at 3:30am, my flight left at 6:25 a.m. and I needed to be leaving for the airport by five. I didn't wake up in time, missed Clinton's 11 phone calls, the call from the driver who brought me to the hotel and Nicole and Kevin's calls I guess it's safe to say I was drunk too. I awoke at 7:34 a.m. HOLLERING and called Clinton right away he knew I over sleep by my screams!

Clinton told me to calm down and hurry and get to the airport so I wouldn't miss the next flight. I called "Southwest" and the operator told me I had to get to the airport before 9:05 a.m. or I would have to pay a change fee. I threw George a bottle of water,

Why Did We Meet? — It Wasn't' By Choice

Love Still Wins

told him to sober up and I punched it to the airport doing 90 mph looking out for the police. I arrived at the airport in time but was flying standby and missed 2 additional flights. I didn't make it back to Atlanta until 3:15 p.m. but overall I really enjoyed myself and every moment was definitely memorable.

* * * * *

My biggest regrets in life are being too damn nice, apologizing when I didn't do anything wrong and making unworthy people a priority. Everybody deserves somebody who makes them look forward to tomorrow. GOD puts people in your life for a reason and removes them from your life for a better reason. Shit happens every day to everyone the difference is how you deal with it. This is why we met and it's not by chance! I stopped waiting for the light at the end of the tunnel and lit that bitch up myself.

The first step to getting somewhere is to decide you are not going to stay where you are. I pray my story can reach many. I pray when I do leave this earth my story will only magnify. We have been taught to keep things a secret and it all goes back to slavery. I'm trying to break many generational curses that have plagued our people for many years. Unfortunately because of this some people will never like me and I will never give a fuck!

By speaking up and making others aware I am breaking the chains. GOD never left me! HE allowed me to go through the valley so I could prevent others from getting lost in it! It took a long time to get here but I made it and I'm never going back to the place where I was before. I learned the issues you don't tackle eventually tackle you. I'm not a preacher but I sure do have a testimony! Won't HE do it!

MESSAGE TO MY MOLESTERS

What you can become depends on what you can overcome. Dust settles, I don't! My past has not defined me, destroyed me, deterred me or defeated me it has only strengthened me. Do not try me, you will not win, GOD made me this tough for a reason. Just like when you have a cold or flu you throw everything you have at it to get better I've done the same with my life! Sometimes you have to chase yourself in order to find yourself. You can either be powerful or pitiful but you can't be both. I won and I told!

I'm coming for what's mine. Nothing more, nothing less!
I TOOK MY POWER BACK!

FIRE FLY'S AND LIGHTING BUGS
By Damion Snowden

One day we'll look back on
Our past lives
When we were lightning bugs
And fireflies.

When we slept all day
And flew all night
And I'll remember following you
Entranced each time you lit up the sky
I'll remember being so inspired by you
That I unknowingly lit my own fire.

Even when they took you
Held you captive
Obedient to your purpose
You still radiated light.
Not even glass jars
Could mar your radiance

But I was saddened and lost
I didn't have your light to follow
In the black sky
But because of you,
Little lightning bugs
And fireflies followed mine.

WE ARE THE GRANDCHILDREN OF THE SLAVES THEY COULDN'T KILL

I learned so much from watching "Roots" for example there's a reason why we don't tell (snitch), turn on each other quickly, sell each other out, produce in mass numbers while sleeping with many women, light skin verses dark skin, loss of respect for one another, and it does take a village to raise a child. All of these things happened and we allowed them to continue over the many, many years and now we have generational curses within our families!

These things bring tears to my eyes and hurt my heart. How in the world do we allow and continue this foolishness?! Why do we focus on issues that don't help us or make us better?! Why can't we unite?!

For my brothers in particular be careful you can't be too bold with these cops I know you're a man don't prove it with your life, prison is Slavery! I learned "They" were slaves too they just never knew it. If I never appreciated the skin I'm in I love my melanin skin and "Roots" made me appreciate it more. My GOD has done so much for me when I was at my weakest HE let me know I was strong when I saw nothing but darkness HE showed me the light when I didn't love myself enough HE loved me more.

I also learned sleeping with someone who's in a relationship knowing they have a mate is wrong on many levels. I've been on both sides of the fence. That was taught to us during slavery because they made us sleep with each other to populate the plantation.

We also have to come out of thinking, "My child is too young to be exposed to knowing about molestation!" When your child learns how to talk is when you should be having the "Good touch Bad touch" conversation. They are never too young to know when someone is touching them inappropriately if you wait until 8 to 12 years old it may be too late!

My grandma never marched because she was living in Gary and the marches for the most part were playing out down south and other cities far from her. My grandmother put in 30 years at a glass company in Illinois all the white women she worked with on the floor were mean, rude or ignored my grandmother unless they needed to have contact with her. Living in Minnesota she went to Red Lobster one time with a friend of hers who is white. The waitress who was white took my grandmother's friend order but never took my grandmothers.

Seeing racism play out today brought back a memory of when I was 10 years old I spoke about this situation in my first book "Eyes Without A Face." My grandmother Minnie who is deceased now, her best friend, her grandson and I went out to eat breakfast at Bob Evans restaurant in Merrillville, Indiana. My grandmother was a nice size woman, when she opened her door to exit the car she hit the car next to hers. There was a white man in the other car and he called my grandmother a fat nigger. My grandmother went into her purse and pulled her gun out. He shut up then and my grandmother told me that day to never let anyone walk over me!

After my grandparent's generation my mother and her siblings experienced racism. My mother and her siblings were born in the 50's and early 60's they stayed on the east side of Gary, Indiana on 14th and Carolina. There were parts of the city they could not go to because they were black.

Today's world in 2016 racism still exists. The racial violence we are seeing and experiencing today is not new it's the cameras that are new. With all the racism going on today I feel like some people have set their clocks back by 300 years. The world needs to know genocide is the deliberate killing of a large group of people especially those of a particular ethnic group or nation. Some of us can relate better to the words of mass murders, mass homicides or a massacre when speaking about genocide.

It's funny how a person paints a dark picture of another in order to paint a "perfect" picture of themselves. For example, a black man named Alton Sterling, is killed by cops and the media prints his prior records. A white teen named Brock Turner rapes a girl and the media prints pictures of him swimming and he only gets 6 months jail time, that's called "White Privilege!" I've learned being black in America is exhausting. Some Caucasians want us to sing, dance, play sports, run fast, be their target practice and be quiet.

I'm lost on why they say "BLACK LIVES MATTER" is a terrorist group. I don't ever recall them burning crosses in anyone's yard, hanging people from trees, terrorizing a specific group of people and spreading hate, are they confusing them with the KKK?! It's like when a white kid shoots up a school the first thing said is "He's mentally ill." Let a black man shoot anybody he's deemed "a thug" after he's killed!
All Tea No Shade

Let's be clear we said, "Black Lives Matter" we never said, "Only Black Lives Matter" That was the media not us. In truth we know "All Lives Matter" we've supported your lives throughout history now we need your help with "Black Lives Matter" for "Blacks Lives" are in danger!

If you're saying "Black Lives Matter" then "ALL Black Lives" should matter to all blacks, if something were to go down like a race war they're not going to pick and choose by skin tone, sexuality or gender when they come for us!

To really understand racism we have to know our history. Facing racism allows us to love our neighbor without looking at the color of their skin but the content of their character. Looking back at my family tree it opened my eyes to racism. It hurt my heart, made me angry and most importantly made me want to join the battle to fight for change. There is no way in this world a specific race should be made slaves or eradicated because of another race's beliefs!

Looking at the world today understanding just how far we have come to know how far we still need to go my great grandmother to the 4th generation Laura Lenoir who was born a slave, died a FREE WOMAN at the age of 113! She "belonged" to the "Bracey family" before her emancipation by the end of the War Between the States.

She lived to see her 14 children and 28 grandchildren assume places of importance in many different fields from education, real estate and law all over the land. She left behind a legacy along with 39 great-grand-children and three great-great-grandchildren.

My great grandmother to the 4th generation was born a slave, I was not, yet I still have restrictions as a free man! I know where I'm headed because I'm destined and covered in HIS blood and no one can take that away from me. America never forgets except when it comes to "slavery and killing unarmed melanted children, women and men!"

We are the grandchildren of the slaves they couldn't kill!

I hold the pen to my story. No one else can hold it. My pen has no eraser and everything is etched in stone! No weapon formed against me shall prosper and the best is yet to come!

www.ingramcontent.com/pod-product-compliance
Lightning Source LLC
Chambersburg PA
CBHW062057290426
44110CB00022B/2618